US Law Simplified

Themes in US Business Immigration Law

Ortega-Medina & Associates

Ed. Orlando Ortega-Medina

CLB Legal
London

Contents

1

US Visa Basics

F oreign individuals (sometimes called "aliens" or "foreign nationals") often require visas to move between countries or to engage in certain activities abroad. Visas are official government endorsements, usually stamped in the applicant's passport at an embassy or consular post, permitting a foreign national to proceed with his plans in the non-native country. Foreign nationals seeking to enter the United States may require either an *immigrant* or a *nonimmigrant* visa. The specific visa required will depend on the individual's needs and goals, as well as his or her status *vis-a-vis* the relevant immigration statutes and regulations.

I. Immigrant Visas

US Citizenship and Immigration Services (USCIS) approves immigrant visa petitions for qualified applicants who wish to enter the US to stay permanently. Once approved by USCIS, the visas themselves are issued by a separate agency known as the US Department of State, usually at US embassies or consular posts located around the world. The specific type of immigrant visa issued will vary depending on the individual's status — such as a family member of a US Citizen or Lawful Permanent Resident; a potential employee of a US company; or a foreign national with business or investment interests in the US.

A. Numerical Limitations on Immigrant Visas

Most immigrant visas are subject to annual numerical limitations. USCIS divides family-sponsored and employment-based visas into limited categories, and grants visas based on a pre-determined allocation among those categories. For example, spouses and children of Lawful Permanent Residents receive a larger percentage of the visas available annually for family-sponsored immigration than do married children of US citizens. The same principle applies to employment-based visas in that "priority workers" (e.g., multinational executives and managers, outstanding professors, and persons of extraordinary ability in various fields) receive a larger proportion of the available employment-based visas than do mere skilled workers.

B. The "Green Card" Lottery

In addition to family-based and employment-based visas, the United States government annually sponsors a Diversity Visa Lottery, commonly known as a "Green Card" lottery. This lottery is intended to increase the diversity of the US population by granting immigrant visas to individuals from countries that historically send few immigrants to the United States. Given that the system involves a lottery, and given that the US government annually receives more than 200,000 entries for only 50,000 available visas, this is a very uncertain method of securing lawful permanent residency in the United States.

C. Immigrant Visas without Numerical Limits

Immigrant visas not subject to numerical limitation are available to:

· Immediate relatives of United States citizens,

· Lawful Permanent Residents returning to the United States following a lengthy period spent abroad, and

· Former American citizens.

The immediate-relative category is the most common of these visa categories even though it covers only spouses, minor children, and parents. USCIS will not grant visas for fraudulent marriages entered into primarily to receive immigration benefits, and penalizes sham marriages through deportation, criminal imprisonment and fines, and permanent bars to permanent residence.

II. Nonimmigrant Visas

Nonimmigrant visas apply to temporary visitors to the United States who intend to return to their home countries. Nonimmigrant admissions far outweigh the number of immigrant visas issued each year. US immigration laws establish a wide range of categories for nonimmigrant visas, and each category brings distinct rights and responsibilities for the visa holder. Some examples of nonimmigrant visa categories include:

· A visas for diplomatic personnel,
· B-1 visas for business,
· B-2 visas for tourism,
· C/D visas for crewmembers,
· F-1 visas for students,
· H visas for temporary workers,
· I visas for foreign journalists,
· J visas for exchange visitors and trainees,
· L1 visas for intracompany transferees,
· O1 visas for aliens of extraordinary ability,
· P visas for artists, musicians and athletes,
· Q visas for cultural exchange visitors, and
· R visas for religious workers.

Some nonimmigrant visas allow the holder to work during his or her stay in the United States. Others enable the visa holder to bring accompanying family members or to enter the country to join US-based family members.

2

ESTA: Electronic System for Travel Authorization to the USA

I n August 2008, the United States Department of Homeland Security (DHS) introduced the Electronic System for Travel Authorization (ESTA), pursuant to which travelers to the United States on the Visa Waiver Program (VHP) are required to seek travel authorization via an online application prior to boarding a carrier. ESTA does not guarantee admission to the United States at a US port of entry; instead, it merely authorizes a traveler to board a carrier destined for the United States.

ESTA travel authorization is required only when a traveler is seeking admission to the US pursuant to VWP, eligibility for which is based on ones country of nationality, not ones country of embarkation. Travelers already in possession of a valid United States visa are exempt from the requirement of obtaining ESTA travel authorization.

Travelers who wish to obtain ESTA authorization should visit the ESTA website at *https://esta.cbp.dhs.gov*; the system will prompt them to enter their biographical and passport information, and to answer the following series of questions:

1. Do you have a physical or mental disorder; or are you a drug abuser

or addict; or do you currently have any of the following diseases (communicable diseases are specified pursuant to section 361(b) of the Public Health Service Act): Cholera, Diphtheria, Tuberculosis infectious, Plague, Smallpox, Yellow Fever, Viral Hemorrhagic Fevers, including Ebola, Lassa, Marburg, Crimean-Congo, Severe acute respiratory illnesses capable of transmission to other persons and likely to cause mortality.

2. Have you ever been arrested or convicted for a crime that resulted in serious damage to property, or serious harm to another person or government authority?

3. Have you ever violated any law related to possessing, using, or distributing illegal drugs?

4. Do you seek to engage in or have you ever engaged in terrorist activities, espionage, sabotage, or genocide?

5. Have you ever committed fraud or misrepresented yourself or others to obtain, or assist others to obtain, a visa or entry into the United States?

6. Are you currently seeking employment in the United States or were you previously employed in the United States without prior permission from the U.S. government?

7. Have you ever been denied a U.S. visa you applied for with your current or previous passport, or have you ever been refused admission to the United States or withdrawn your application for admission at a U.S. port of entry?

8. Have you ever stayed in the United States longer than the admission period granted to you by the U.S. government?

9. Have you traveled to, or been present in Iran, Iraq, Libya, North Korea, Somalia, Sudan, Syria or Yemen on or after March 1, 2011?

Contrary to popular myth, not all arrests or convictions must be disclosed. Instead, only arrests, cautions, or convictions that "resulted in serious damage to property, or serious harm to another person or government authority" or that relate to "possessing, using, or distributing illegal drugs" need be disclosed. Determination of whether a particular arrest or conviction (or any other negative contact with law enforcement) falls under one of these enumerated categories can only be made by testing it against the relevant controlling US statutes and case law. As such, it is strongly recommended that any intending traveler to the United States who has suffered a negative contact with law enforcement, regardless of where it happened or how long ago it occurred, and regardless of whether it is considered "spent", should consult with an experienced US immigration lawyer before actioning an ESTA application for travel authorization.

Direct contact with either USCIS or the US Embassy regarding the issue of prior arrests or convictions is discouraged, as the customer service representatives of both of these agencies often instruct individuals with prior law enforcement matters (regardless of the category) to apply for a visa, which will significantly delay ones travel and may unnecessarily sully one's permanent record with irrelevant matters that need not have been disclosed in the first place.

Travelers who plan on seeking ESTA authoization should action their online applications at least 72 hours in advance of their planed travel, as some ESTA applications may take up to 72 hours to process.

Once a traveler applies for ESTA, one of the following responses should appear in short order:

1. Authorization Approved: Travel authorized.
2. Travel Not Authorized: Traveler must obtain a nonimmigrant visa at a US Embassy or Consulate before traveling to the US
3. Authorization Pending: Traveler will need to check the ESTA Web site for updates within 72 hours to receive a final response.

Once approved, ESTA travel authorization is valid for multiple entries into the United States for up to two (2) years, or until the traveler's passport expires, whichever comes first. However, travelers must update their itineraries and US destinations on the ESTA website as they are planned.

As the system is electronic, travelers are not required to carry a paper copy of their travel authorization; however, carrying a paper copy is nonetheless recommended, and travelers should ensure they keep a record of their ESTA application number.

After 12 January 2009, any traveler who does not apply for ESTA or is not authorized before traveling may be denied boarding, experience delayed processing, or be denied admission at a US port of entry.

If an ESTA application is not approved ("Travel Not Authorized"), a traveler may reapply after a period of 10 days; however, unless the traveler's circumstances have changed significantly, ESTA will likely be denied again. A traveler whose ESTA application is denied *must* obtain a visa in an appropriate category from a US embassy or consulate before he or she may travel to the United States.

US embassies and consulates are unable to provide the reason why ESTA authorization was denied. The ESTA website provides a link to the DHS Travel Redress Inquiry Program (TRIP); however, there are no guarantees that a request for redress via TRIP will resolve the denial.

Additional notes on ESTA:

- Travelers that are only transiting through the United States must still obtain authorization through ESTA. "In transit" should be entered as the address in the United States.
- Citizens of Bermuda, Canada, the Marshall Islands, and Micronesia do not need to apply for ESTA.
- The ESTA application fee is currently $14.00 for approved applications and $4.00 for denied applications.

- ESTA authorization is not required of travelers seeking to enter the United States via a land border.
- Entering false information into ESTA may render a traveler permanently ineligible for future travel to the US.
- Although an ESTA authorization is valid for two years, a new application is required if a traveler subsequently suffers a visa refusal, a denial of entry, removal or deportation, or any negative contact with law enforcement that renders him or her inadmissible, or if he or she travels to Iran, Iraq, Libya, North Korea, Somalia, Sudan, Syria or Yemen.

3

Common US Visa and Immigration Myths

The law firm of Ortega-Medina & Associates often receives inquiries from HR Professionals regarding employees who have suffered United States immigration consequences due to their reliance on erroneous information found on the Internet. While much information found on the internet may be accurate, we are aware of an abundance of *visa myths* arising out of incorrect information perpetuated across the internet on sites ranging from chat boards to government information pages.

Unfortunately, these *visa myths* often lead to legal consequences of varying degrees, including, for example: a.) A foreign employer may send one of its employees to the United States mistakenly believing the employee is authorized to carry out certain business activities that are, in fact, prohibited by law, leading to refusals of entry, visa denials, or worse; or b.) A businessperson may forego applying for a specific visa category that would otherwise allow him or her to establish a profitable business in the United States, due to a mistaken belief that he or she is ineligible for the category.

The fact of the matter is that United States immigration law is rarely, if ever, straightforward—and it is important to distinguish between the reality and the myths. In this article, therefore, we address nine (9) visa myths most commonly brought to our attention by our clients, in the hopes of helping HR Professionals and individuals engaged in cross-border business activities to avoid costly missteps.

Myths Associated with Short-Term Business Activities

Myth 1: "We need to send one of our employees to the United States to do some work on our behalf. Our employee will not be paid by a United States company and will stay only for a short period of time; therefore, she may enter on the Visa Waiver Program/ESTA."

The Reality: The Visa Waiver Program does not authorize productive work, regardless of where the business traveler's employer is located, or regardless of whether or not the business traveler is paid for his work. This same rule also applies to individuals holding a standard B-1 *Business Visitor* visa. The business activities allowed under the Visa Waiver Program and standard B-1 Business Visitor visa include, but are not limited to, attendance at business meetings, conferences, seminars, and exhibitions. However, conducting leadership and management training seminars, or other training events, is not authorized on the Visa Waiver Program.

It is important to be entirely clear on whether your employee's business activities are authorized under the Visa Waiver Program. If your employee performs unauthorized work in the United States, he may be removed from the United States or refused entry to the United States on a future trip. Your employee may thereafter be unable to travel to the United States on the Visa Waiver Program, even as a tourist, and may face problems in securing a B-1 Business Visitor's visa in the future. Such personal legal consequences could potentially lead to a claim by the employee against the employer that sent her to the United States, as the employee may assert she made the trip under pressure.

Within the B-1 visa regulations, there are special subcategories of B-1 visas that, when granted, allow different types of productive work. The most common of these subcategories is a *Special Business Concession* (also known as *B-1 in lieu of H visa*) that allows qualifying individuals to perform productive work in the United States on behalf of a foreign employer. Employers generally find applications for the *Special Business Concession visas* to be less onerous compared with more traditional visa categories as the application is presented directly to the United States Embassy or Consulate abroad. However, the visa application must clearly demonstrate the employer's need to send the applicant to the United States, as well as the applicant's qualifications establishing his or her eligibility for the Special Business Concession category, and must conform with the frequently changing procedural requirements of the US Department of State. We recommend that you consult with a US-qualified immigration attorney if you wish to pursue this option for one of your employees, given that a failed visa application, even through a simple misstep, may also render the applicant permanently ineligible to travel on the Visa Waiver Program.

Myths Associated with L1 Intracompany Transfers

Myth 2: "Our company's United States affiliate must be trading for at least one (1) year before we can transfer one of our employees on an L1 visa."

The Reality: This is not the case under the L1 "New Office" regulations. These regulations allow individuals employed by an affiliated company abroad in a managerial, executive, or specialized knowledge capacity to be transferred to a brand new United States company to commence the operations of the company.

The L1 visa under the "New Office" regulations will be issued for up to one (1) year initially, and the sponsoring company must demonstrate in its petition that the transferee will be in a position to step away from any duties in the set-up of the company that are not strictly managerial, executive, or that do not require specialized knowledge, by the end of year one (1).

A reverse version of this myth suggests the transfer may occur even before the establishment of the United States affiliate. In actuality, whilst an L1 visa may be issued to a transferee prior to the actual commencement of operations, USCIS must be satisfied in reviewing the visa petition that there is an already-established United States entity prepared to receive the transferee in formal "bricks and mortar" business premises. To facilitate the visa process, our law firm often assists foreign companies in this initial formation and establishment of the United States entity, which we handle in conjunction with the preparation of the L1 visa petition to avoid unnecessary delays.

Myth 3: "The candidate we would like to move to the United States is paid as an independent contractor, not as an employee. Hence, she is not eligible for an L1 transfer to our United States affiliate."

The Reality: The candidate may still be eligible for the L1 visa category. Contractors that work exclusively for the foreign company, but are paid as contractors for tax reasons, may still be transferred to the affiliated United States company on an L1 visa if they are otherwise eligible. During our initial consultation with an employer, we analyze the current and prospective roles to ensure that these qualify for the L1 category under the relevant laws and regulations. If the candidate does not meet the requirements for the L1 visa category, there are often other visa options available.

Myths Associated with Company Registration under an E2 Treaty

Myth 4: "Our company must invest at least $250,000 USD in the United States to be eligible for registration under the E2 Treaty category, in advance of any E2 Employee Transfers."

The Reality: Not necessarily. The US Department of State ("DOS"), the United States government agency that adjudicates E2 company registrations, does not set a minimum investment figure. Instead, the rules state that the investment must be *substantial*. The dollar figure required for a *substantial* investment depends on the nature of the business to be started or purchased. Your company's investment must represent a substantial proportion of the total value of the business to be purchased, or it must be sufficient to start up a profitable new business.

Our firm has handled successful E2 registration applications for companies investing as little as $50,000 USD when this was the total amount required to start up the business to the point of operation. Following successful registration of the company with the DOS, E2 Employee transfers can be arranged quickly and at relatively low cost, as compared with categories such as L1 or H1B.

Myth 5: "Our director may apply for E2 visas to allow her to travel to the United States to invest in the creation of an affiliate or branch office."

The Reality: This is not correct. *Before* one may legally apply for an E2 visa, the investment of money, goods or intellectual property must be completed, and commercially at risk. Certain regulations do allow travelers to visit the United States pursuant to the B-1 category for the purpose of making E2 qualifying investments. However, such matters must be handled carefully to ensure that the activities the investor carries out are authorized under the relevant United States immigration rules. For example, the investor will not be eligible to actively manage the United States enterprise, or otherwise work in the United States enterprise, until the relevant embassy or consular unit approves the subject E2 registration application and has issued the corollary E2 visa. Similarly, the officer at the port of entry may refuse the investor entry to the United States or, worse yet, administratively deported unless he or she is satisfied that the investor will only engage in those activities authorized by the E2 viva category.

US Business Immigration law firms customarily work with companies at the initial stage of their expansion to the United States. They will typically offer services to review the proposed investment activities in the United States and to provide documents for presentation at the port of entry in support of the investor's proposed activities in the United States, in anticipation of a future E2 application.

Myths Associated with Arrests, Cautions, and Convictions

<u>Myth 6</u>: "Our employee has a criminal record. He is therefore required to apply for a visa before traveling to the United States."

<u>The Reality</u>: It depends on the particular applicant's record. This myth most commonly arises in relation to Question 2. on the *Electronic System for Travel Authorization* ("ESTA") required to travel to the United States. Question 2 asks:

Have you ever been arrested or convicted for a crime that resulted in serious damage to property, or serious harm to another person or government authority?

When one answers "<u>yes</u>" to Question 2, US Customs and Border Protection reviews the application and determines whether it will authoize travel or whether the traveler must apply for a visa at a United States embassy or consulate abroad before traveling to the United States.

The portion of the question that generally causes confusion is whether the arrest or conviction was one which resulted in '*serious damage to property*' or '*serious harm to another person*'. The guidance notes for Question 2 indicate that the terms '*serious damage to property*' and '*serious harm to another person*' equate to the United States legal term of art '*crime involving moral turpitude*' ("CIMT"), which is even more confusing to the layperson. Common law in the United States defines moral turpitude ambiguously as 'conduct which is inherently base, vile, or depraved, and contrary to the accepted rules of morality and the duties owed between persons or to society in general.' Furthermore, the punishment imposed does not shed any light as to the presence or absence of moral turpitude. For example, some crimes punishable by only a fine may be considered crimes involving moral turpitude, while other crimes generally considered by the general public to be serious are not.

The determination as to whether a 'foreign arrest or conviction' involves moral turpitude requires a comparison of the subject criminal record against *both* the equivalent United States Federal or State criminal statutes and the relevant United States immigration laws. We recommend that you consult with a qualified US immigration lawyer before instructing the subject employee to complete the ESTA questionnaire or contacting the United States Embassy or Consulate to schedule an appointment for a visa application. The United States Embassy or Consulate do not advise in advance as to whether it considers a particular arrest or conviction is a CIMT. Only a qualified US immigration lawyer will be able to provide insight into this in advance of the consular appointment and will be able to assess the likelihood of success in such an application.

It is quite common for an individual that legally *could* have answered "no" to Question 2, to nevertheless book a visa interview, either because he is uncertain about the definition of CIMT, or because he directly consults with the DOS call center and is instructed to do so. At the visa interview, even if the attending officer is unable to find that the arrest, caution or conviction is a CIMT, she may nevertheless deny the visa application on other grounds, such as "medical inadmissibility" in the case of a Drink-Drive arrest, or for the less comprehensible "insufficient ties outside of the United States". A visa denial on these grounds will render the individual who would have otherwise received ESTA approval unable to travel on the Visa Waiver Program. Furthermore, the visa denial remains on one's DOS record for life and is quite difficult to overcome in a future application as Embassy officials typically defer to the previous denial unless there has been a material change of circumstances.

Myth 7: "Our employee's criminal conviction is now spent (or expunged), so he does not need to disclose it to the US Immigration Service or to the Embassy of the United States."

The Reality: The United States government does not recognize the concept of spent convictions. An arrest or conviction that falls under a category requiring disclosure must always be revealed regardless of how long ago it occurred and regardless of whether it has been removed from one's record.

Other General Immigration Myths

Myth 8: "Once one has spent several years in the United States on a non-immigrant visa, one is automatically eligible to receive a "Green Card" (i.e., Legal Permanent Resident status).

The Reality: Unlike many countries, an individual does not automatically become eligible for Lawful Permanent Resident ("LPR") status after living in the United States for a certain number of years. The United States grants LPR status following approval of a sponsored petition or application process that is separate and distinct from the non-immigrant visa process.

These sponsored petitions may be lodged by qualifying US employers, or by certain United States citizen or LPR family members. A number of different categories exist to petition for LPR status, and each category maintains its own requirements and timescales. These categories normally face higher scrutiny and more requirements by USCIS than nonimmigrant petitions, and it is wise to consult with a qualified United States Immigration Lawyer before commencing the process.

Myth 9: "Our employee has remained in the United States for the full 90-days authorized by the Visa Waiver Program, but is not yet ready to leave. Hence, we will fly her out for the day so that she will be able to stay on for another 90 days when she re-enters the United States."

The Reality: Maybe. Each time one seeks to enter the United States, a US Customs and Border Protection ("CBP") officer determines one's eligibility to enter the United States and, if admitted, how long one may stay. Lengthy stays of more than a few weeks and particularly stays for the entire ninety (90) days followed by a quick return to the

United States may arouse the suspicion of CBP. Re-entering the United States after a full ninety (90) day stay and brief departure is not strictly prohibited, but a port officer may nevertheless deny one's entry based on suspicions that the visitor will not leave by the expiration date recorded on her electronic I-94 Record of Admission, that she will engage in unauthorized productive work while in the United States, or that she intends to permanently reside in the United States.

One should always discuss one's need to keep an employee in the United States for more than ninety (90) days with a qualified US immigration attorney to determine if there is a visa that may help facilitate their travel to the United States throughout the year. It is also wise to consult with an accountant or a tax advisor familiar with United States taxation as the individual may be subject to United States tax liability after remaining in the United States for more than 180 days in the aggregate in any given year – even on the Visa Waiver Program.

Conclusion

These are just a handful of the visa and immigration myths that abound in the public domain, including on internet forums and chat rooms. Reliance on these myths can lead to serious negative conse-quences, including unnecessary visa denials, invalidation of one's right to enter the United States on the Visa Waiver Program, loss of money and business opportunities and even removal or deportation from the United States. Even if you intend to handle your company's visa or immigration matter on a DIY basis, it is best to consult with an experienced US immigration lawyer – if only to confirm your understanding of the relevant US immigration laws and regulations. Seeking professional advice will minimize the danger of misstepping as you attempt to navigate the US immigration minefield.

4

Allowable Business Activities under VWP versus Special Business Concession Visa under the FAM

One of the questions that our law firm receives most often from our business clients is, "What constitutes a proper business activity under the Visa Waiver Program?" This question is most often posed by the businessperson who intends to carry out employment activities on behalf of his or her foreign employer, but who is unable to identify an applicable visa category. The truth is that the business activities that are allowed under the Visa Waiver Program (VWP), are quite limited and circumscribed, and attempts to enter the United States to carry out activities that exceed these limits often result in a refusal of admission.

The purpose of this article is twofold: a.) to more precisely identify those business activities that are permissible under the VWP; and b.) to specify the various special concessions contained in the relevant regulations that will allow certain individuals to access the United States for employment purposes on behalf of their foreign employers via a specially annotated nonimmigrant visa.

I. Allowable Business Activities under the VWP or on a Standard B-1 Visa

Individuals who desire to enter the United States for business purposes, and who are otherwise eligible for visa issuance, may be classifiable as nonimmigrant B-1 visitors. The business activities contemplated by the B-1 visa classification generally entail activities *other than the performance of skilled or unskilled labor*. Thus, the issuance of a B-1 visa is not intended for the purpose of obtaining and engaging in employment whilst in the United States. Specific circumstances or past patterns have been found to fall within the parameters of this classification and are listed below.

It can be difficult for the layperson to distinguish *between* appropriate B-1 business activities *and* business activities that constitute skilled or unskilled labor in the United States, which would *not* be appropriate for one holding B visa status. The clearest legal definition comes from the decision of the Board of Immigration Appeals (BIA) in Matter of Hira (Interim Decision 1647, 1966), affirmed by the Attorney General.

The Hira matter involved a tailor measuring customers in the United States for suits to be manufactured and shipped from outside the United States. The decision stated that this was an appropriate B-1 activity, because the principal place of business and the actual place of accrual of profits, if any, was in the foreign country. Most of the following examples of proper B-1 business activities are drawn from, and relate to the Hira ruling, in that they relate to activities that are incidental to work that will principally be performed outside of the United States.

As set out in the US Department of State's Foreign Affairs Manual, Aliens should be classified B-1 visitors for business, if otherwise eligible, so long as they are traveling to the United States to do one or more of the following:

1. Engage in commercial transactions, which do not involve gainful employment in the United States (such as a merchant who takes

orders for goods manufactured abroad);
2. Negotiate contracts;
3. Consult with business associates;
4. Litigate;
5. Participate in scientific, educational, professional, or business conventions, conferences, or seminars; or
6. Undertake independent research.

The statutory terms of the Immigration and Nationality Act (INA 101(a)(15)(B)) specifically exclude from this classification aliens coming to the United States to perform skilled or unskilled labor. Aliens seeking entry to the United States for the purpose of engaging in employment activities, which do not fall under the A, C, D, E, G, H, I, J, L, O, P, Q, or NATO visa categories must be classified as immigrants, and, consequently, will be excluded from the United States unless they are in possession of a corresponding valid immigrant visa.

II. Special Business Concession Visa Annotations under the FAM

Chapter 9 of the United States Foreign Affairs Manual (9 FAM) identifies specific special concessions for aliens who may be eligible for B-1 business visas, but who intend to exceed the *Hira* list of permitted business activities, provided they meet the criteria of one of the non-exhaustive categories listed below. (Note: An individual who normally accesses the United States via ESTA Travel Authorization should make a special application to the Department of State with regards to any of the following special concession categories.)

1. Members of Board of Directors of US Corporation

An alien who is a member of the board of directors of a US corporation seeking to enter the United States to attend a meeting of the board or to perform other functions resulting from membership on the board.

2. Investor Seeking Investment in the United States

An alien seeking investment in the United States, including an investment that would qualify him or her for status as an E-2 treaty investor. Such an alien is precluded from performing productive labor or from actively participating in the management of the business prior to being granted E-2 status.

3. Aliens Normally Classifiable as H-1 or H-3 (i.e. "in lieu of H")

There are cases in which aliens who qualify for H-1 or H-3 visas may more appropriately be classified as B-1 visa applicants in certain circumstances; e.g., a qualified H-1 or H-3 visa applicant coming to the United States to perform H-1 calibre services on behalf of their foreign (non-US) employer or to participate in a training program.

In such a case, the applicant *must not* receive any salary or other remuneration from a United States source other than an expense allowance or other reimbursement for expenses incidental to the alien's temporary stay. It is essential that the remuneration or source of income for services performed in the United States continues to be provided by the applicant's foreign employer, and that the alien meets the following criteria:

- With regard to foreign-sourced remuneration for services performed by aliens admitted in this category, where a United States business enterprise or entity has a separate business enterprise abroad, the salary paid by such foreign entity shall not be considered as coming from a "US source;"
- In order for an employer to be considered a "foreign firm" the entity must have an office abroad and its payroll must be disbursed abroad. To qualify for a B-1 visa, the employee must customarily be employed by the foreign firm, the employing entity must pay the employee's salary, and the source of the employee's salary must be abroad; and
- An alien classifiable H-2 shall be classified as such notwithstanding

the fact that the salary or other remuneration is being paid by a source outside the United States, or the fact that the alien is working without compensation (other than a voluntary service worker classifiable B-1). A nonimmigrant visa petition accompanied by an approved labor certification must be filed on behalf of the alien.

4. Personal Employees of Foreign Nationals in Nonimmigrant Status

A personal or domestic employee who accompanies or follows to join an employer who is seeking admission into, or is already in, the United States in B, E, F, H, I, J, L, M, O, P, or Q nonimmigrant status, must meet the following requirements:

a) The employee has a residence abroad which he or she has no intention of abandoning (notwithstanding the fact that the employer may be in a nonimmigrant status which does not require such a showing);

b) The employee can demonstrate at least one year's experience as a personal or domestic employee;

c) The employee has been employed abroad by the employer as a personal or domestic employee for at least one year prior to the date of the employer's admission to the United States;

OR

If the employee-employer relationship existed immediately prior to the time of visa application, the employer can demonstrate that he or she has regularly employed (either year-round or seasonally) personal or domestic employees over a period of several years preceding the domestic employee's visa application for a nonimmigrant B-1 visa;

a) The employer and the employee have signed an employment contract which contains statements that the employee is guaranteed the minimum or prevailing wages, whichever is greater, and free room and board, and the employer will be the only provider of employment to the employee;

b) The employer must pay the domestic's initial travel expenses to the

United States, and subsequently to the employer's onward assignment, or to the employee's country of normal residence at the termination of the assignment.

5. Personal/Domestic Employees of US Citizens Residing Abroad

Personal or domestic employees who accompany or follow to join US citizen employers who have a permanent home or are stationed in a foreign country and who are visiting the United States temporarily. The employer-employee relationship must have existed prior to the commencement of the employer's visit to the United States.

6. Personal/Domestic Employees of US Citizens on Temporary Assignment in the United States

a. Personal or domestic employees who are accompanying or following to join US citizen employers temporarily assigned to the United States provided that:

1) The employee has a residence abroad which he or she has no intention of abandoning;

2) The alien has been employed abroad by the employer as a personal or domestic servant for at least six months prior to the date of the employer's admission to the United States;

3) In the alternative, the employer can show that while abroad the employer has regularly employed a domestic servant in the same capacity as that intended for the applicant;

4) The employee can demonstrate at least one year of experience as a personal or domestic servant by producing statements from previous employers attesting to such experience; and

5) The employee is in possession of an original contract, or a copy of the contract, to be presented at the port of entry, which contains the original signatures of both the employer and the employee.

b. The US citizen employer is subject to frequent international transfers lasting two years or more as a condition of the job as confirmed by the employer's personnel office and is returning to the United States for a stay of no more than four years. The employer will be the only provider of employment to the domestic employee and will provide the employee free room and board and a round trip airfare as indicated under the terms of the employment contract; and

c. The required employment contract has been signed and dated by the employer and employee and contains a guarantee from the employer that, in addition to the provisions listed in item (b) above, the employee will receive the minimum or prevailing wages whichever is greater for an eight-hour work-day. The employment contract shall also reflect any other benefits normally required for US domestic workers in the area of employment. The employer will give at least two weeks notice of his or her intent to terminate the employment, and the employee need not give more than two weeks notice of intent to leave the employment.

7. Personal Employees/Domestics of Lawful Permanent Residents (LPRs)

Personal employees of all lawful permanent residents (LPRs), including conditional permanent residents and LPRs who have filed an Application to Preserve Residence for Naturalization Purposes, must obtain permanent resident status, as it is contemplated that the employing LPR is a resident of the United States.

8. Professional Athletes

Professional athletes, such as golfers and auto racers, who receive no salary or payment other than prize money for his or her participation in a tournament or sporting event.

Athletes or team members who seek to enter the United States as members of a foreign-based team in order to compete with another sports team shall be admitted provided:

a. The foreign athlete and the foreign sports team have their principal place of business or activity in a foreign country;

b. The income of the foreign-based team and the salary of its players are principally accrued in a foreign country; and

c. The foreign-based sports team is a member of an international sports league or the sporting activities involved have an international dimension.

d. Amateur hockey players who are asked to join a professional team during the course of the regular professional season or playoffs for brief try-outs. The players are draft choices who have not signed professional contracts but have signed a memorandum of agreement with a National Hockey League (NHL)-parent team. Under the terms of the agreement, the team will provide only for incidental expenses such as round-trip fare, hotel room, meals, and transportation. At the time of the visa application or application for admission to the United States, the players must provide a copy of the memorandum of agreement and a letter from the NHL team giving the details of the try-outs. If an agreement is not available at that time, a letter from the NHL team must give the details of the tryout and state that such an agreement has been signed.

9. Yacht Crewmen

Crewmen of a private yacht who are able to establish that they have a residence abroad which they do not intend to abandon, regardless of the nationality of the private yacht. The yacht is to sail out of a foreign home port and cruising in US waters for more than 29 days.

10. Horse Races

An alien coming to the United States to perform services on behalf of a foreign-based employer as a jockey, sulky driver, trainer, or groomer.

11. Outer Continental Shelf (OCS) Employees

a. The Outer Continental Shelf Lands Act Amendments of 1978 (OCSLA) were enacted on September 18, 1978. 43 USC. 1356 of OCSLA directs, that with specified exceptions, all units operating on the Outer Continental Shelf (OCS) must employ only US citizens or lawful permanent resident (LPR) aliens as members of the regular complement of the unit. Subsequently, the US Coast Guard issued regulations (33 CFR 141), which became effective on April 5, 1983. The regulations contain guidelines concerning exemptions available to units operating on the OCS.

b. Not included are nonmembers of the regular complement of a unit such as specialists, professionals, or other technically trained personnel called in to handle emergencies or other temporary operations, and extra personnel on a unit for training or for specialized operation; i.e., construction, alteration, well logging, or unusual repairs or emergencies.

12. Ministers of Religion Exchanging Pulpits

Ministers of religion temporarily exchanging pulpits with US counterparts who will continue to be reimbursed by the foreign church and will draw no salary from the host church in the United States.

13. Missionary Work

Members of religious denominations, whether ordained or not, entering the United States temporarily for the sole purpose of performing missionary work on behalf of a denomination, so long as the work does not involve the selling of articles or the solicitation or acceptance of donations and provided the minister will receive no salary or remuneration from US sources other than an allowance or other reimbursement for expenses incidental to the temporary stay. "Missionary work" for this purpose may include religious instruction, aid to the elderly or needy, proselytizing, etc. It does not include ordinary administrative work, nor should it be used as a substitute for ordinary labor for hire.

14. Applicant Who Are Unable to Otherwise Qualify for R Status

In cases where an applicant is coming to perform voluntary services for a religious organization, and does not qualify for R status, the B-1 status remains an option, provided that the applicant meets the requirements in 9 FAM 41.31 N9.1, even if he or she intends to stay a year or more in the United States.

15. Participants in Voluntary Service Programs

a) Aliens participating in a voluntary service program benefiting US local communities, who establish that they are members of, and have a commitment to, a particular recognized religious or nonprofit charitable organization. No salary or remuneration should be paid from a US source, other than an allowance or other reimbursement for expenses incidental to the volunteers' stay in the United States.

b) A "voluntary service program" is an organized project conducted by a recognized religious or nonprofit charitable organization to assist the poor or the needy or to further a religious or charitable cause. The program may not, however, involve the selling of articles and/or the solicitation and acceptance of donations. The burden that the voluntary program meets the Department of Homeland Security (DHS) definition of "voluntary service program" is placed upon the recognized religious or nonprofit charitable organization, which must also meet other criteria set out in the DHS Operating Instructions with regard to voluntary workers.

III. Other Business Activities Classifiable as B-1

While the categories listed below generally may be classified under the proper applicable nonimmigrant class, i.e., A, E, H, F, L, or M visas, the US Department of State may issue properly annotated visas to otherwise eligible aliens under the criteria provided below.

I. Commercial or Industrial Workers

a. An alien coming to the United States to install, service, or repair commercial or industrial equipment or machinery purchased from a company outside the United States or to train US workers to perform such services. However, in such cases, the contract of sale must specifically require the seller to provide such services or training and the visa applicant must possess specialized knowledge essential to the seller's contractual obligation to perform the services or training and must receive no remuneration from a US source.

b. These provisions do not apply to an alien seeking to perform building or construction work, whether on-site or in-plant. The exception is for an alien who is applying for a B-1 visa for supervising or training other workers engaged in building or construction work, but not actually performing any such building or construction work.

II. Foreign Airline Employees

Foreign airline employee aliens who:

(1) Seek to enter the United States for employment with a foreign airline that is engaged in international transportation of passengers and freight;

(2) Are working in an executive, supervisory, or highly technical capacity; and

(3) Otherwise meet the requirements for E visa classification but are precluded from entitlement to treaty trader E-1 classification solely because there is no treaty of friendship, commerce, and navigation in effect between the United States and the country of the aliens' nationality, or because they are not nationals of the airline's country of nationality.

III. Employees of Foreign Airlines Coming to the United States to Join Aircraft

Employees of foreign airlines coming to the United States to join aircraft may also be documented as B-1 visitors in that they are not transiting the United States and are not admissible as crewmen. Such applicants, however, must present a letter from the headquarters branch of the foreign airline verifying their employment and the official nature of their duties in the United States.

IV. Clerkship

Except as in the case described below, aliens who wish to obtain hands-on clerkship experience are not deemed to fall within B-1 visa classification.

a.) Medical Clerkship: An alien who is studying at a foreign medical school and seeks to enter the United States temporarily in order to take an "elective clerkship" at a US medical school's hospital without remuneration from the hospital. The medical clerkship is only for medical students pursuing their normal third or fourth year internship in a US medical school as part of a foreign medical school degree. (An "elective clerkship" affords practical experience and instructions in the various disciplines of medicine under the supervision and direction of faculty physicians at a US medical school's hospital as an approved part of the alien's foreign medical school education. It does not apply to graduate medical training, which is restricted by 212(e) and normally requires a J-visa.)

V. Business or Other Professional or Vocational Activities

An alien who is coming to the United States merely and exclusively to observe the conduct of business or other professional or vocational activity may be classified B-1, provided the alien pays for his or her own expenses. However, aliens, often students, who seek to gain practical experience through on-the-job training or clerkships must qualify under INA 101(a)(15)(H) or (L), or when an appropriate exchange visitors program exists (J).

VI. Participants in Foreign Assistance Act Program

An alien invited to participate in any program furnishing technical information and assistance under section 635(f) of the Foreign Assistance Act of 1961, 75 Statute 424.

VII. Peace Corps Volunteer Trainers

An alien invited to participate in the training of Peace Corps volunteers or coming to the United States under contract pursuant to sections 9 and 10(a)(4) of the Peace Corps Act (75 Statute 612), unless the alien qualifies for A classification.

VIII. Internship with United Nations Institute for Training and Research (UNITAR)

Participants in the United Nations Institute for Training and Research (UNITAR) program of internship for training and research who are not employees of foreign governments.

IX. Aliens Employed by Foreign or US Exhibitors at International Fairs or Expositions

Aliens who are coming to the United States to plan, construct, dismantle, maintain, or be employed in connection with exhibits at international fairs or expositions may, depending upon the circumstances in each case, qualify for one of the following classifications.

X. Foreign Government Officials

Aliens representing a foreign government in a planning or supervisory capacity and/or their immediate staffs are entitled to "A" classification if an appropriate note is received from their government, and if they are otherwise properly documented.

XI. Employees of Foreign Exhibitors

Employees of foreign exhibitors at international fairs or expositions who are not foreign government representatives and do not qualify for "A" classification ordinarily are classified B-1.

XII. Employees of US Exhibitors

While alien employees of US exhibitors or employers are not eligible for B-1 visas they may be classifiable as H-1 or H-2 temporary workers.

IV. Special Cases

I. Artists and Entertainers

a. Except for the following cases, B visa status is not appropriate for a member of the entertainment profession (professional entertainer) who seeks to enter the United States temporarily to perform services. Instead, performers shall be accorded another appropriate visa classification, which in most cases will be P, regardless of the amount or source of compensation, whether the services will involve public appearance(s), or whether the performance is for charity or US based ethnic society.

b. The term "member of the entertainment profession" includes not only performing artists such as stage and movie actors, musicians, singers and dancers, but also other personnel such as technicians, electricians, make-up specialists, film crew members coming to the United States to produce films, etc.

c. A professional entertainer may be classified B-1 if the entertainer:

(1) Is coming to the United States to participate only in a cultural program sponsored by the sending country;

(2) Will be performing before a nonpaying audience; and

(3) All expenses, including per diem, will be paid by the member's government.

d. A professional entertainer may be classified B-1 if the entertainer is coming to the United States to participate in a competition for which there is no remuneration other than a prize (monetary or otherwise) and expenses.

e. An artist coming to the United States to paint, sculpt, etc. who is not under contract with a US employer and who does not intend to regularly sell such art-work in the United States.

II. Still Photographers

The Department of Homeland Security (DHS) permits still photographers to enter the United States with B-1 visas for the purpose of taking photographs, provided that they receive no income from a US source.

III. Musicians

An alien musician may be issued a B-1 visa, provided:

(1) The musician is coming to the United States in order to utilize recording facilities for recording purposes only;

(2) The recording will be distributed and sold only outside the United States; and

(3) No public performances will be given.

IV. Medical Doctors Observing and Consulting with Colleagues

A medical doctor otherwise classifiable H-1 as a member of a profession whose purpose for coming to the United States is to observe US medical practices and consult with colleagues on latest techniques, provided no remuneration is received from a US source and no patient care is involved. Failure to pass the Foreign Medical Graduate Examination (FMGE) is irrelevant in such a case.

V. H-3 Trainees

a. Aliens already employed abroad, who are coming to undertake training and who are classifiable as H-3 trainees. Department of Homeland Security (DHS) regulations state that in order for an alien to be classifiable as H-3, the petitioner must demonstrate that:

(1) The proposed training is not available in the alien's own country;

(2) The beneficiary will not be placed in a position which is in the normal operation of the business and in which citizens and resident workers are regularly employed;

(3) The beneficiary will not engage in productive employment unless such employment is incidental and necessary to the training; and

(4) The training will benefit the beneficiary in pursuing a career outside the United States.

b. They will continue to receive a salary from the foreign employer and will receive no salary or other remuneration from a US source other than an expense allowance or other reimbursement for expenses (including room and board) incidental to the temporary stay. In addition, the fact that the training may last one year or more is not in itself controlling and it should not result in denial of a visa, provided the consular official is satisfied that the intended stay in the United States is temporary, and that, in fact, there is a definite time limitation to such training.

V. *When an Advisory Opinion is Required*

Even though the above-noted categories are quite specific, there are some cases that defy categorization. In such cases, the US State Department is required to request an Advisory Opinion (AO) prior to the issuance of a B-1 visa in any case involving temporary employment in the United States. An AO is required in these cases to ensure uniformity and to avoid the issuance of a B-1 to an alien subject to the safeguards of the petition and labor certification requirements.

5

NAFTA and the Management Consultant Dilemma

I t is a common scene, repeated over and again at the various US–Canada border posts. A young Canadian executive approaches an officer of the United States Department of Homeland Security, and hands her a small pile of documents prepared for him by the HR Manager of his prospective employer.

"I'm here to apply for a TN visa," declares the applicant.

"In what category?"

"Uh...Management Consultant."

The immigration officer glances at the documents with an air of distaste and tells the applicant to take a seat. Thirty minutes later the officer calls the applicant into an office and subjects him to a grueling hour of cross-examination.

"What is this?" demands the officer, shoving a piece of letterhead in his face.

The applicant peers at the document. "It's a letter from the company that wants to hire me."

"It's too short and doesn't describe a management problem," says the officer, tossing aside the letter and pulling out another document.

"How about this?"

"That's my resume," answers the applicant, his face turning red.

"Uh, huh..." says the officer. "Just what are you trying to pull here?"

"What do you mean?" asks the applicant.

"You're no Management Consultant. You don't have any management experience."

And so on...

The result: Denial of the TN application. The reason: Either the position or the applicant does not qualify for the *Management Consultant* designation. The consequences: Lost time, lost money, loss of a potentially valuable employee, loss of a lucrative job opportunity, and humiliation.

The Management Consultant Category - An Incorrectly Perceived Loophole

As most people involved in HR Management are aware, the North American Free Trade Agreement (NAFTA) has simplified the placement of certain Canadian professionals into high-demand jobs in the United States. As long as the candidate fits into the cookie-cutter professional categories listed in Appendix 1603.D.1 of the NAFTA, the interested company is able to avoid the longer processing times and higher fees associated with the H-1B visa.

Most of the NAFTA categories require at least a bachelor's degree. And as long as the candidate can prove he or she has the required education, approval of a TN visa is virtually assured. For example, a Canadian Engineer with a bachelor's degree should have no trouble qualifying for a position as an Engineer with a US company.

A few NAFTA categories, however, allow for the substitution of work experience in place of the required bachelor's degree. One of these is the *Management Consultant* category, which allows "five years of experience as a management consultant, or five years experience in a field of specialty related to the consulting agreement" to substitute for a missing bachelor's degree.

Unfortunately, the *Management Consultant* category is incorrectly perceived by many HR Managers as a sort of "loophole" in the immigration law which allows them to place well-qualified candidates who have not completed a formal degree program, but who are otherwise qualified for the position offered because of their experience in the subject field.

Thus, HR Managers frequently send non-degreed persons such as computer professionals with no management experience to the border, allegedly to accept a job in the States as a *Management Consultant*; or they send non-degreed candidates with management experience to the border, with the intent of placing them in long-term management positions with US companies. Applications such as these are invariably doomed to failure.

Why the Management Consultant Designation is So Difficult to Obtain

USCIS Free Trade Officers are well aware of the misperceptions that exist regarding the *Management Consultant* category. They adjudicate and deny countless bogus TN applications in this category on a daily basis. As such, whenever someone presents at a US-Canada border with a TN application seeking admission through the *Management Consultant* category, the officer's guard immediately goes up.

While it is difficult for the officer to deny a TN visa when the applicant has at least a bachelor's degree, it is fairly easy to question whether a non-degreed applicant's experience is "relevant" to the *Management Consultant* position offered. It is important to understand that US immigration law gives its Free Trade Officers complete and unfettered discretion to make a decision on a NAFTA visa application. Denials are not appealable. So, when Free Trade Officers have an opportunity to use this discretion, they do so...sometimes with a vengeance.

Make no mistake: the Free Trade Officer will go through every word of a TN application, compare the applicant's CV with his or her past-employment reference letters to spot any contradictions, and analyze the sponsoring company's cover letter and financial statements. Finally, the officer will thoroughly grill the applicant with respect to his or her claimed prior experience as well as about the proposed duties of the proffered job with the sponsoring company. Given USCIS Free Trade Officers' generally negative predisposition toward the *Management Consultant* category, these applications do not tend to hold up well under such close scrutiny.

So, What Exactly is a Management Consultant Anyway?

Contrary to the belief of most HR Managers, a *Management Consultant* (for purposes of United States immigration law) is not a manager. A *Management Consultant* is a consultant to management hired by an organization to help solve a particular short-term management problem. Free Trade Officers view these consultants as "hired guns": they are hired to solve a particular problem, and then, having completed their work, they must get out. Offers of company benefits such as retirement and 401K plans, stock options, and life insurance are inconsistent with this view. These types of benefits are all trappings of a permanent employee, not a temporary "hired gun".

Therefore, at minimum, the company's cover letter to USCIS should state with particularity the management problem to be solved, the reason for the short-term need for an outside consultant, how the applicant is qualified to solve the problem, and the terms of compensation. The application should also include a detailed CV which documents at least five full years of relevant experience, as well as detailed reference letters from all past employers consistent with the CV. Contradictions between any of the above documents will be duly noted by the Free Trade Officer, and will likely result in the denial of a TN visa.

The Effect of Past Denials

All is not lost if a TN visa is denied by a Free Trade Officer. That same complete and unfettered discretion wielded by one Free Trade

Officer empowers the next officer to re-consider an application as if presented for the first time, if the officer wishes to do so. Because of this, it is entirely possible for an applicant to be refused by one officer at Niagara Falls in the morning and admitted by another officer at Pearson International Airport in the afternoon, *without any change to the application.* However, we do not recommend the latter approach, because some officers will perceive the same-day reapplication as an attempt to play the system.

Our firm has successfully assisted a myriad of individuals who have been refused once, twice or even three times. (Of course, the more times one has been refused, the more difficult the case becomes.) Our task as experienced immigration lawyers is the same in all of these cases: a.) Perform a comprehensive evaluation of the Applicant and the Proposed Employment; b.) Selection of the Proper Visa Category; and c.) Assembly of the most USCIS-Friendly Visa Application Possible.

Some *Recommendations*

It is always better for all parties concerned if, instead of trying to handle important immigration matters on their own, HR Managers and potential TN applicants take the time to consult with an immigration professional prior to applying for a visa. The savings in time, money and frustration are well worth the investment. However, if they insist on handling these delicate cases on their own, it is helpful to keep the following in mind:

1. A *Management Consultant* is a hired gun—a consultant to management, hired to solve a short-term management problem;
2. A Management Consultant should not be compensated over and above the base salary;
3. A non-degreed applicant must have a minimum of five complete years of verifiable experience as a consultant to management or in a field of specialty related to the consulting agreement. Make sure

you have the documents to prove all five years;

4. There should be no discrepancies whatsoever between any of the documents presented to the Free Trade Officer;

5. The applicant should be prepared to answer intelligently, and in detail, the officer's questions regarding: a.) the applicant's past experience, and b.) the management problem he or she is being hired to solve;

6. A TN application must be made in conjunction with an "entry". So, the applicant should not be instructed to drive to the border in advance to see if the officer will issue the visa; and finally

7. Always remember that Free Trade Officers have complete and unfettered discretion to rule on NAFTA cases. Therefore, the applicant should present with as deferential an attitude as possible.

6

Introduction to the L1 Visa

There is a special visa available for companies that wish to expand operations into the United States by opening a branch, a warehouse or an office. This visa, known as the L1 visa, is one of the most popular — especially since it may lead to fast-track permanent residency for its executives and managers — and is relatively easy to obtain with the right documentation and presentation. The requirements are:

I. Company Requirements

The foreign company must have been in operation for at least one year and must remain in operation at all times after the opening of the United States division;

A *qualifying organization* may include a branch of the same employer, or a parent, subsidiary, or affiliate;

New offices must submit additional evidence, including a business plan, and must show progress on start-up activities after one year.

The annual sales volume or gross revenues of the foreign company ideally should exceed $250,000 (relative to the exchange rate of local currency and the cost of doing business in the subject foreign country);

Ideally, the foreign company should employ at least 3 individuals in executive, managerial or professional positions;

One must be able to demonstrate that the foreign company is success-ful, in good standing, financially solid, that expansion into the United States will not negatively affect its foreign operations, and that the expansion will eventually create jobs for locally-employed workers in the United States.

II. Categories of Workers Eligible to be Transferred to US Operation

Executives - Includes the President, Vice-President, Secretary, or Treasurer of the company

Professional Managers - Should be General Managers, Sales Managers, Production Managers, etc. (First-line supervisors generally do not qualify).

Specialized Knowledge Workers - Must have unique and special knowl-edge specific to the product or the company, not generally acquirable in the open labor market.

III. Personal Requirements

The visa applicant must have worked for the foreign company for at least 1 out of the last 3 years; and

The visa applicant's presence in the United States is essential to the success and the smooth operation of the United States company.

The initial duration of the visa is for 1 year for a new office, or 3 years for transfer to an established subsidiary, with possible extensions of additional 2 years, to a maximum of 7 years for managers and executives, and 5 years for specialized knowledge workers. An applicant who has resided in the United States for the maximum visa period must reside abroad for a full year before being readmitted in the same status.

IV. Processing Time, Government Fees

Government processing is rapid compared to other business visa categories—15 days or less with premium processing—because there is no need to file either an Application for Labor Certification or a Labor Condition Application. And government filing fees are relatively low,

41

compared with other visas—just $1,820.00 USD including premium processing. [Note: Processing for citizens of CANADA is completed on a same-day basis at most CANADA-US ports of entry or at the US "pre-flight clearance" office located at most international airports in CANADA.]

Following the first year of trade by the US entity, it may petition for permanent residency for its <u>qualifying managers and executives,</u> without the need to test the job market through the labor certification process.

V. Business Expansion Visa (L-1A) v. Treaty Investor (E-2)

It is often the case that one may qualify for either the Treaty Investor (E-2) or Business Expansion (L-1A) visa. The question then arises as to which of the two visas is the most advantageous. Following is our analysis of this question:

The L-1A Business Expansion visa has the following distinct **disadvantages**:

a.) The initial validity period is only for 1 year compared with 5 years for an E-2 visa;

b.) The total time allowable in the United States in the L-1 category is 7 years for an L-1A and 5 years for an L-1B, after which one must depart from the country for at least 1 full year, whereas the E-2 visa is granted in 5-year increments and is indefinitely renewable;

c.) As of the time of this article, government filing fees for L-1 cases average $3000 USD per each L-1 visa compared with only $205 USD for an E-2 visa; and

d.) One applies for L-1 visas on a one-off basis, meaning that each application is a new application and credit is not given to evidence previously submitted for the sponsoring company, whereas an initial E-2 visa stands as an evidentiary paradigm against which additional follow-on E-2 visas can be turned around within a couple of weeks.

As for the commonly-held view that one may not upgrade from E-2 visa to permanent residency (i.e., a "Green Card"), this is true *only* in the case where there is no foreign company related to the E-2 registered entity. Fast-track permanent residency in the EB1C category, in fact, may indeed be available to E-2 executives or managers under the same rules as those holding L-1A status.

7

Avoiding Common Pitfalls Relating to Employee Transfers

Whave often heard it suggested that when immigration lawyers recommend that laypersons avoid filing their own immigration paperwork, financial self-interest is the only motivation. This is far from the truth. We cannot estimate how many times our firm has had to try and undo the damage done to a perfectly good case by an overconfident immigrant, human resources manager, or placement agency. Personally, I would rather lose a potential client to another lawyer than to see her take a chance on filing her own paperwork with USCIS. The likelihood of failure is just too high.

Following is a list of five notable immigration horror stories that have come across our desk since the beginning of the year. All of these sad situations could have been avoided if the parties would have first consulted with an experienced immigration lawyer.

The L-1 Transfer That Almost Never Happened

The CEO of a UK Software company based in Manchester called me at the end of April. She had been trying since December 2006 to transfer three key employees to a US subsidiary in the Southwestern United States. Two of these were British citizens, and one was a citizen of a country in

Southeast Asia. This should have been a straightforward case.

The company's US partner attempted to handle the paperwork himself, since he'd previously handled two NAFTA visas for a pair of Canadian professionals. What the company did not know was that the application requirements and procedures for a NAFTA visa differ significantly from those applicable to the L-1 intracompany transferee visa. Although the partner had all the information and documents he needed to process the case in January, he held up the petitions so that he could research the correct L-1 procedures. It was late April, and the partner still had not moved forward on the petitions.

I asked the CEO to courier me the information and documents. Within three weeks of receiving the documents, we were able to send all three of the transferees to the United Embassy in London to have their passports stamped with their L-1A visas. Problem solved.

The Consular Denial

An artists agent/promoter was trying to bring a group of Peruvian folk musicians to the US for a series of music festivals. Amazingly, he was able to correctly prepare and file the required petition. He received the approval notice from USCIS within 45 days. When the musicians went to the US Consulate in Lima to pick up their visas, they were denied. The problem: The consular official didn't believe the musicians had "sufficient ties to Peru", despite the fact they had lived all their lives in Peru, their parents, wives and children lived in Peru, and they had jobs and businesses to return to in Peru once the visas expired.

Having previously dealt with quite a few consular denials, we got on the telephone with the US consular official who had dealt with the musicians, made a list of all his objections, and reprocessed the visa applications. Within a week, the musicians were issued their visas, and were on their way to California. (Incidentally, prior approval of a visa petition by USCIS does not guarantee issuance of the visa by the US State Department; and prior issuance of a visa by the US Consulate does not guarantee admission to the US by USCIS.)

Missing the H-1B Boat

Toward the end of February we received a call from an exasperated young man who had been offered a job at a medical clinic in Nevada as a medical physicist. After some independent research on the internet, he had determined that the clinic should file an H-1B petition on his behalf. The company, which had never petitioned for an alien worker before, left the immigration details up to him.

He studied USCIS website, downloaded the forms, and sent them to the clinic. The clinic filled out the forms and sent them into USCIS with a filing fee of $190.00. That was in January, and he still had not heard anything from USCIS. The source of his stress was the rumor that began circulating in February that the H-1B cap for the current fiscal year would be reached on April 2, 2007 — the very first day that the visa cap was slated to open. He wanted to know what would happen if his application was not approved before the cap was reached.

Before dealing with his primary concern, we asked him to fax us all the documents the clinic had filed with USCIS. Our worst suspicions were confirmed, upon review of the documents. The forms had been filled out incorrectly, forms that did not have to be filed had been filed along with the correct forms, and the filing fee was incomplete. The prevailing wage for the position had not been determined, and no labor condition application had been filed with the Department of Labor. Additionally, the clinic had not provided enough evidence regarding either the clinic or the position offered. Besides all of this, USCIS regulations were clear that petitions that reached its mailroom prior to April 2, 2007 would be rejected. Thus, it was clear to us that USCIS would eventually reject the petition. When we gave the young man the bad news, he was quite skeptical. We suggested that he pull back the original petition, and re-file a corrected petition exactly on April 2, 2007. He told us he would think about it and call us back.

On March 14, we received another call from the young man. USCIS had rejected the petition as we had predicted and had returned it to the clinic. He asked us to take over the case. On April 2, 2007, we filed the corrected H-1B petition. Over 150,000 petitions arrived at USCIS on the same day, all of them vying for the 65,000 available visas. Fortunately, our client's H-1B visa petition was among those randomly selected for processing. He has since received his Notice of Approval.

The NAFTA Rejection

On May 25, 2007, we received a telephone call from a woman who had been hired as a computer systems analyst by a high-tech startup company in San Francisco. She had landed the job through a recruiting firm in Toronto. That same recruiting firm had referred the candidate to a Canadian lawyer to prepare the application. This should have been a fairly routine matter, since the woman qualified for a TN-1 visa under the North American Free Trade Agreement (NAFTA). However, it turned out that the lawyer had limited experience in these matters. In his apparent ignorance, the lawyer sent the woman to the US/Canadian border at Buffalo with a poorly prepared application package (which lacked sufficient evidence of the woman's qualifications) to apply for the visa in advance of the date she actually planned to enter the United States. She was rejected.

We reviewed the paperwork she had presented at the border, and found it to be quite wanting in substance as well as presentation. She asked us to take over the case, and in a matter of five days, we sent her off to the pre-flight inspection post at Pearson International Airport with an expertly prepared application, and her bags in hand. Happily we received a telephone call from her that afternoon giving us the good news that she had been issued the TN-1 visa and was about to board her flight to San Francisco. We have received several referrals from this client in the last two months.

It's Never as Easy as They Tell You

In early April of this year, our office was contacted by a gentleman who had been offered a high-paying job as a family counselor in the Southern United States. Although he had no University Degree, he had acquired just short of four years experience in this field. He contacted USCIS on his own and was told by some unnamed clerk that all he needed to do was to fill out "an I-750", present it at the airport, then file a petition for an adjustment of status once he arrived in the United States.

Thrilled at the news, the gentleman returned to Canada, sold his home, quit his job (as did his wife) took his children out of school, and they all showed up at the airport, bags in hand. Of course, they were turned away. Reasons: 1.) he had followed the wrong procedure for a permanent work visa; 2.) he didn't qualify under any temporary work visa category since he did not hold a university degree and did not have at least 5 years experience in the relevant area.

Unfortunately, there was nothing we could do for this gentleman, since he did not qualify for any type of visa. Even though he stood a good shot at qualifying for a visa under NAFTA with one more year of experience, he had already quit his job and sold his house. The damage was done.

Not every case can be salvaged, as the above example illustrates. But many can, and we are quite proud of the cases we have successfully shepherded to a satisfactory disposition. Of course, it would be much better for all parties concerned if, instead of trying to handle important immigration matters on their own, potential immigrants or employers take the time to consult with an experienced immigration lawyer. The savings in time, money and frustration is well worth the investment.

8

What To Do When You Receive an RFE: The Dos and Don'ts

Receipt of a Request for Evidence ("RFE") from UCSIS is the first sign that your visa or immigration case is in trouble. In most cases, an RFE signifies that you have not properly addressed the legal requirements underpinning the visa category for which you have applied. In some cases, it can mean that USCIS discovered contradictory or inconsistent information when it compared the various supporting documents you submitted as against the forms and covering letter, or as against information in the public domain. And in other cases, it can mean that the visa category you selected was not the correct visa category for your particular circumstances. In any case, receipt of an RFE requires prompt action to avoid an outright denial of your visa petition.

I. Understanding the Structure of an RFE

Generally, an RFE consists of 4 sections:

- Section 1 quotes from the statutes, regulations and case law relevant to the requirements underpinning the visa category you have

selected;
- Section 2 summarizes your visa petition, and will include some reference to the supporting evidence that you submitted;
- Section 3 is USCIS' explanation of how (in the view of the Reviewing Officer) you have failed to satisfy the legal requirements summarized in Section 1 of the RFE;
- Section 4 lists the specific information and documents that you must provide to satisfy USCIS that you meet the minimum legal requirements for the subject visa category.

Do not ignore or merely skim Section 1, because a clear understanding of the legal requirements is critical to properly respond to an RFE. It is likewise essential that you do not start to assemble the responsive documents until after you have a very clear understanding of USCIS' reservations about the visa petition as it was originally constituted. This means that you should revisit your original submission, and carefully compare it to what USCIS is alleging in its RFE.

If you find that USCIS misunderstood your original submission, it may simply be that the evidence was not presented in an easy-to-understand format. In any case, once you clearly comprehend where the problem lies with your petition, you should map out your plan of action so as to strategize how you will respond to the RFE.

II. Responding to an RFE

You may find that some (if not all) of the information and documentation that USCIS requests in its RFE was already been submitted with your initial petition. Typically, the immediate reaction to this is to shoot back an angrily worded response asking USCIS to refer back to the original submission. This approach, in the author's view, is a mistake and likely to result in a denial. Instead, the author's experience has shown that it is best to expand on the originally submitted documentation, and to update the record from the point of submission, rather than quarrel with USCIS.

At the end of the day, there are two (2) ways to respond to an RFE:

· Respond with exactly what was requested; or
· Withdraw the petition.

Responding with anything other than what was requested invites a denial of the petition. On the other hand, responding with exactly what was requested will usually result in an approval of the petition. Be very careful that the additional evidence you submit is completely consistent with the information and documentation in the original petition. If any changes have occurred since the original filing that affect your documentation (e.g., employee turnover) you must ensure that these changes are explained in your response.

If you find that you are unable to produce all of the requested documentation, or if you find that you are unable to satisfy the legal requirements of the selected category, then you have the option of withdrawing the petition without prejudice and trying again – either with a new, improved submission; or with an application in an alternate visa category. The advantage to withdrawing your petition without prejudice has the benefit of avoiding a denial on the record. However, before withdrawing your petition you should make sure that the Beneficiary will not be left without a visa status.

III. What to do in the event of a denial of your Petition

In the event USCIS denies your petition after it reviews your *Response to RFE*, this is not the end of the road. The law provides the following remedies:

1. *Administrative Review of Denial* for Premium Processing customers;

2. *Motion to Reopen; and*

3. *Appeal to either the Administrative Appeals Office of USCIS* (or, in some case, to the *Board of Immigration Appeals*).

Given that there are strict deadline for filing any of these remedies, and given that a thorough knowledge of the applicable law and procedure is essential to the success or failure of these remedies, it is well worth consulting with a seasoned US Immigration Appellate Lawyer before proceeding with any of them.

IV. The Importance of Obtaining a Second Opinion

The preparer of the original visa petition is not always the best person to review and respond to an RFE. Instead, it is often recommendable to have one's visa submission reviewed independently in conjunction with the RFE, to allow for maximum objectivity in strategizing a response.

9

L1 Visa Renewal Challenges

Ortega-Medina & Associates has conducted a thorough review of selected published decisions in which L1 visa renewal petitions were denied. Following is a discussion of the elements common to most of these cases.

The L1 visa is one of the most popular vehicles by which the owners of foreign businesses can obtain permanent status in the United States by expanding operations to the United States. The process is carried out in three steps:

First, the initial L1 visa is issued for a period of one year to set up operations of the new US branch;

Second, the L1 visa must be renewed based (in part) on the first-year record of the US branch;

Third, once renewed, for an additional 2 years, the L1 visa holder may apply for permanent residency with the support of the US branch.

It would not be an exaggeration to state that USCIS often approves the initial L1 visa on a vision—supported by a well-drafted business plan and a convincing amount of money in the bank. However, if getting ones foot in the door seems easy enough, renewal of the visa frequently turns out to be a nightmare for the applicant who—more often than not—has uprooted hearth and home with the intention of permanently relocating to the United States.

Our firm has surveyed a select number of published decisions by the Administrative Appeals Unit of the Department of Justice in which USCIS denied a petition for L1A visa renewal. In 98% of these cases the reasons for the denial were virtually identical:

1. The petitioner did not establish that the beneficiary will be employed in a primarily managerial or executive capacity;
2. The petitioner did not employ adequate or sufficient personnel.
3. The petitioner did not establish physical offices;

The biggest mistake most applicants and/or their immigration lawyers make is to assume that the same duties that supported the initial visa petition will be sufficient to support the renewal. This assumption is fatal to a renewal case. This is because the duties an L1A beneficiary must undertake in the first year to set-up operations must include – by necessity – non-managerial and non-executive essential functions such as administration, marketing, public relations, and human resource management.

USCIS is mindful that such non-qualifying duties are required to get the new operation off the ground. However, the applicable regulations grant a company only one year to accomplish this. By the time the renewal petition must be filed, these non-managerial and non-executive duties must have been transferred to locally employed personnel, working in actual physical offices. The size of the staff is not important; only that it be adequate to cover the afore-mentioned essential functions.

In a typical case, this issue comes to light when the company or its lawyer receives a request for additional evidence (an "RFE") from USCIS. The RFE usually requests a very detailed accounting of the beneficiary's duties, a detailed organizational chart showing the names of all individuals employed by the US company, as well as a detailed accounting of their duties, and payroll and tax records proving the locally employed employees.

Upon receipt of the RFE, some companies try to remedy the lack of essential personnel by quickly engaging a few people solely to satisfy the RFE, or they attempt to justify the use off-shore personnel to cover these functions. A review of the published denials, however, reveals that such quick-fix attempts are a reason, in and of themselves, for the denial. Such quick-fixes simply serve to demonstrate that the new company has not reached the level of development required at the one-year mark. In short, a petitioner that finds itself at the receiving end of an RFE questioning whether the beneficiary will be employed in a primarily managerial or executive capacity should seriously consider other visa options.

In our opinion, the wisest course is to plan a renewal strategy as part of your initial case preparation. Aside from being a sound business practice, this course of action will go quite far to avoid any unpleasant and potentially catastrophic surprises in the future.

10

Introduction to the E2 Visa

The E2 visa is a special non-immigrant visa available to nationals of treaty countries entering the US to do the following:

a.) Develop and direct the operations of an enterprise in which they have invested, or are actively in the process of investing a substantial amount of capital;

b.) Invest substantially in an already-established US enterprise;

c.) Develop and direct investments from the treaty country.

The investment should create job opportunities for US workers. While it is preferable to have the US workers hired at the time of application for the treaty investor visa, reasonably achievable projections of jobs that will be created in the future is often sufficient.

There is no specific dollar amount that must be invested to meet the substantial amount requirement, but the investment must meet one of two tests:

1. It must represent a significant proportion of the total value of the business enterprise; or

2. It must be sufficient to establish a profitable and viable business of

the type contemplated.

Family members (spouses and unmarried children under 21) of the principal Treaty Investor visa holder may obtain derivative status that allows them to live, work and attend school in the US.

Treaty Investor visas are generally issued for five years, although some consulates issue the first visa for two years. Extensions are generally unlimited as long as the investment continues, and are often reissued for five additional years at a time.

Applicants in this category must have extensive documentation detailing the business plan, the amount of the investment, the nature of the capital, and calculation of jobs to be created. A successful visa application will also demonstrate how the proposed enterprise will benefit the United States.

Treaty Investor (E-2) v. Business Expansion Visa (L-1A)

It is often the case that one may qualify for either the Treaty Investor (E-2) or Business Expansion (L-1A) visa. The question then arises as to which of the two visas is the most advantageous. Following is our analysis of this question:

The Business Expansion visa has the following distinct advantages:

1. One does not have to invest a specific amount of cash in advance of visa approval;

2. Once the case is presented, one can have approval in as little as 7 - 10 days;

3. Adjudication of the case takes place in the US, rather than at the relevant US Embassy or Consulate (which can be quite tough on investor cases);

4. The spouse of the principal gets a general work permit during the life of the visa;

5. Eligibility for Priority Permanent Residency in the US after 1 year.

In contrast, as explained above, the Treaty Investor visa requires the investment of a "substantial" amount of money, in advance of approval, and usually requires adjudication at an American Embassy or Consulate, which can take several weeks.

Also, although one may plan to remain in the US for only a few years, one might very well change one's mind about this at some point in the future; the Treaty Investor visa does not generally lead to Permanent Residency regardless of the amount of time one spends in the US, with some exceptions for certain multinational executives and managers.

11

Frequently Asked "E" Visa Questions and Answers

Treaty Investor visas ("E-2" visas) to the United States are authorized on the basis of treaties between the United States (US) and approximately sixty other countries. The US Embassy in London is responsible for processing E visas for all of the United Kingdom.

Following are common questions that we frequently receive from nationals of the United Kingdom regarding this very popular visa.

Q. *Do I actually need an E visa to reside in the United States if I already own a US business?*

A. Unless you are a US Citizen or a US Green Card holder, you must be in possession of a valid have a visa in order to enter the United States in Treaty Trader or Treaty Investor status. Further, all successful E visa applicants and their dependents are expected to present valid passports in order to be issued the visa, regardless of nationality.

Q. *I am a citizen of the United Kingdom residing in Spain. May I lodge an E-2 visa application at the US Embassy in Madrid?*

A. To qualify for an E-2 Treaty Investor Visa, citizens of the United Kingdom must actually reside in the United Kingdom (with some exceptions), and proof of this must be submitted as part of the E-2 registration and application process.

Q. *I am a citizen of Australia presently residing in the United Kingdom. Must I lodge my E-2 visa application in the United Kingdom or in Australia?*

A. A citizen of one of the other qualifying treaty countries who is resident in the United Kingdom may lodge an E visa application at the US Embassy in London. The relevant treaty either may or may not allow one to lodge an application in ones home country. In the case of a citizen of Australia, filing in Australia is permitted and may save significant processing time. By contrast, a citizen of Spain residing in the United Kingdom is not presently allowed to file an E-2 visa application in Spain. You should consult with a competent US immigration lawyer for more details about this issue.

Q. *I received a change of status in the United States from US Citizenship and Immigration Services (USCIS). Is that all that I need to present in order to be issued an E visa at the US Embassy or US Consulate?*

A. No. The change of status simply allows you to remain in the United States until the expiration of the status granted. If you have been granted a change of status by USCIS and leave the US, you must have an E visa in your passport in order to return to the US in that status. To obtain a visa you must lodge a complete application with the appropriate US Embassy or US Consulate. Adjudication of your case can vary from two weeks to six months, depending on which US Embassy or US Consulate is deciding your case.

Q. *How much money do I need to invest?*

A. There is no minimum amount for an investment. E-2 visa regulations state that the investment must be sufficient to ensure success of the business. As different types of businesses require different amounts of capital, the amount you will need to invest depends on your US enterprise.

Q. *Do I really have to invest the money before I apply for the visa? Can't the United States government issue me the visa first?*

A. E-2 visa regulations state that the funds must be "irrevocably committed" to the investment before the visa may be issued. Therefore, you must document that your investment meets this criteria at the time of initial application; this is usually accomplished by showing that the investment has already been made. Funds can be considered to be irrevocably committed, however, if they are held in an escrow account solely contingent on the issuance of an E visa.

Q. *Must the business be trading at the time I lodge my E-2 visa application?*

A. Yes. The relevant E-2 visa regulations state that the enterprise must be "real and active". Most US Embassies and consular posts interpret this to mean that the business must be actively trading at the time your E-2 visa application is lodged.

Q. *How can I possibly start a business if I don't have the visa?*

A. You may enter the United States in B-1 (temporary business) visa status in order to set up (not run) your business. You may not be paid in the US while in B-1 status. If your enterprise requires someone to manage or run daily operations, you may hire individuals who are already properly documented to work in the US prior to receiving your visa. Once you have the initial commitments completed, you should apply immediately for the E visa.

Q. *How long do I have to wait before I can apply for a "green card" or US citizenship?*

A. An E visa is a non-immigrant visa and does not lead to either a "green card" or US Citizenship. You may remain in the US only as long as your business conforms to E visa regulations, assuming you maintain proper visa and immigration status.

Q. *Do I need an immigration attorney?*

A. There is no legal requirement that you hire an attorney to lodge your E visa application. While many E Visa applicants choose to retain the services of an attorney to aid in the preparation of their case, others do not. It is to your advantage, however, to engage the services of a competent immigration attorney or law firm that is fully familiar with the specific procedures observed by the US Embassy or US Consulate in your home country. Failure to observe these procedures will certainly result in significant time delays, may seriously prejudice the outcome of your case, and may result in irreversible financial consequences.

Q. *Where can I get information about good places to invest in the US?*

A. Please contact our office for more information.

Q. *What licenses and permits do I need to open and run a business in the United States?*

A. Licensing and permit requirements vary by state and county and with the type of business you wish to operate. For specific information, you should contact the appropriate government offices in the locality where you plan to start your business. Alternatively, you may retain the services of a law firm to make the required inquiries on your behalf.

Q. *I already own an E company and want to employ someone who is not in the US Can employees of an E company qualify for an E visa to work in my US enterprise?*

A. To qualify for an E visa as the employee of an E company, the applicant must have the same citizenship as the owners of the E company. Additionally, the job to be performed must be executive or supervisory in nature, or the employee must possess skills which are essential to the operation of the US enterprise.

Q. *Can my spouse and children work in the US?*

A. Effective January 16, 2002, dependent spouses of E visa holders are eligible to apply for work authorization from USCIS. Children of E visa holders are not permitted to work in the United States unless they independently qualify for employment authorization, such as an E, H, or L visa.

Q. *My spouse (or child) uses a different surname than I do. Is that a problem?*

A. A dependent whose surname differs from the surname of the E visa holder should have on-hand proof of the relationship (a marriage certificate for spouses or birth certificates for children, for example).

Q. *Can my fiancé(e), common law or same-sex partner accompany me?*

A. Under US immigration law, a legal marriage must exist before one is considered to be a spouse. Therefore, fiancé(e)s, common law or unmarried same-sex partners do not qualify for derivative E visa status. Other avenues may be available to assist those applicants in such a situation. Please contact our firm for more details.

Q. *My spouse and/or children are citizens of a country other than my own. Can they still accompany me?*

A. The spouse and children (defined as unmarried and under 21 years of age) do not need to have the same citizenship as the principal applicant. However, dependents of E visa holders are required to have visas in order to accompany the principal applicant to the US

Q. *Will I have to appear before the US Embassy or US Consulate in person?*

A. For all categories of visas, including Treaty Visas, each applicant age 14 or older must appear for a personal interview before a Consular Officer. In all cases, each applicant (including those under 14 years of age), must be physically present in the country of application at the time of issuance. Those applicants who are found to be ineligible for a US visa for criminal convictions, immigration violations, drug charges, or other similar reasons may have to appear to determine grounds of ineligibility and applicability of a waiver for any such ineligibility. In such cases the applicant must be prepared for a wait of up to 180 days weeks while eligibility is confirmed and/or a waiver requested.

Q. *How long does the processing normally take?*

A. Processing times vary greatly between the various US Embassies and US Consulates. For example, the US Embassy in Mexico City can process an E-2 visa case in one week, while the US Embassy in London can take up to 6 months to process a case. Generally speaking, if your initial submission is not complete, then your case will not be officially "received" or it may be kicked back to allow you to provide the missing information. Upon resubmission of the case, it will generally be placed at the back of the processing queue. Please note that frequently an applicant's submission will require clarification or additional information before the adjudicating officer can make a determination of eligibility. If this is the case, you (or your attorney of record) will be notified in writing.

Q. *Will it speed up the processing if I send my passport to the US government at the time that I lodge my application?*

A. No. You should not send passports until it is requested by the US Embassy or US Consulate. Submitting passports early can delay the processing of your case.

Q. *I paid $100.00 when I applied. Why is there an additional fee for issuance?*

A. The $100.00 fee you paid at the time of application is called the Machine-Readable Visa (MRV) processing fee. This non-refundable fee is charged to all applicants for non-immigrant visas regardless of whether the application is approved. Once your case has been approved, there may be an additional fee for issuance of the visa. This fee is called a "reciprocity fee" and is determined by the fees that your country of citizenship charges US citizens for similar visas. The E visa reciprocity fee for a Canadian citizen, for example, is currently $40.00.

Q. *I've read all this information, and I still have questions. Who can answer them?*

A. We recommend that you consult with a US immigration attorney local to you in your country of residence.

12

The E2 Visa: A Stepping Stone to EB5

While the EB-5 Immigrant Investor Visa is a great option for foreign nationals wishing to obtain US permanent residency, the increased length in processing time posted by USCIS have some investors looking for a quicker path to living and working in the United States. For foreign nationals interested in making a direct EB-5 investment in their own business, the E-2 Treaty Investor Visa is a viable path to the EB-5 visa, and eventual permanent residency.

However, using the E-2 visa as a stepping-stone for ones green card through the EB-5 visa is not a suitable option for all immigrant investors. The EB-5 visa has two distinct paths for investment. The first path is the traditional direct investment. In this instance, the immigrant investor would develop and direct his or her own EB-5 business. The investor would be responsible for meeting the EB-5 immigration requirements, including job creation requirements and other EB-5 compliancy issues.

The second path for securing an EB-5 visa is through the indirect Regional Centre investment. Immigrant investors looking to take advantage of an EB-5 project located in a USCIS approved Regional Centre are considered passive investors. Their money is pooled together with other foreign investors to fund a larger new commercial enterprise.

Typically, a client investing through a Regional Centre does not have control over the day-to-day operations of the project, and has little or no ownership interest in the business.

Immigrant investors interested in a Regional Centre project would not be suitable candidates for using the E-2 visa as a stepping-stone for the EB-5 visa. For those who prefer the direct EB-5 path, allowing them to create and direct their own business, the E-2 visa may serve them well, provided they meet the other requirements.

Who qualifies for the E-2 visa? Unfortunately, not all potential immigrant investors qualify for the E-2 visa. The E-2 visa is available for nationals of a treaty country who wish to gain admittance to the United States through a substantial investment in a US business. However, not all countries maintain the specific treaty with the United States required for eligibility. For example, nationals of Russia and China (not including Taiwan) are not eligible to apply under the E-2 Treaty Investor Visa. A list of eligible countries can be found on the US Department of State website.

Further, the investor must be seeking to enter the United States to develop and direct the new business. As a result, the investor must prove at least 50% ownership interest in the new business. If approved, the E-2 investor should receive a non-immigrant visa valid for a period of up to five years. This visa can be renewed indefinitely provided certain requirements are met.

How can the E-2 visa lead to a Green Card via the EB-5 visa? With proper planning and guidance from an immigration attorney, one may structure ones E-2 business to facilitate an EB-5 investment in the future. Once a foreign national has an approved E-2 business, he or she may invest additional funds into the company and apply for the EB-5 visa once the requirements have been met. During the adjudication of ones EB-5 investor visa, one may remain in the United States on ones E-2 status and continue to develop and direct the business.

For example, Mario Rossi, a national of Italy, is interested in obtaining a Green Card through the EB-5 program. He currently runs a successful pasta sauce production company in Italy and is interested in expanding his business in the United States. He has a net worth of $1,000,000 USD and is willing to put forth approximately $250,000 USD to fund his new US venture. He expects to generate significant profit by year five. He has been advised by his immigration attorney that a successful EB-5 business located in a Targeted Employment Area (TEA) requires a minimum investment of $500,000 USD. Further, the current processing times for an EB-5 visa are approximately 16 months.

While Mr. Rossi is able to invest $500,000 USD, he is nervous about making such a significant investment contribution before obtaining an approved visa. He is also keen to move to the United States quickly, and is unwilling to wait 16 months while the EB-5 visa is being adjudicated.

After further consulting with his legal counsel, Mr. Rossi applies for an E-2 visa based on his newly established pasta sauce production company, *XYZ Pasta Sauce Inc.* in the United States. He is subsequently approved for a five-year E-2 visa after investing $250,000 USD in the US company.

After living in the United States and working at *XYZ Pasta Sauce Inc.* for three years, he feels the company is growing more rapidly than expected, and wishes to expand the business. Mr. Rossi invests an additional $250,000 USD into the company and instructs his attorney to file for the EB-5 visa. Mr. Rossi continues to live and work in the United States while his EB-5 petition is pending with USCIS.

After a year and a half, Mr. Rossi's EB-5 petition is approved. He briefly returns to Italy to obtain his immigrant visa at the US Embassy in Rome, and upon returning to the United States he receives his permanent resident card.

What are the possible benefits of applying for an E-2 visa before the EB-5 visa? Perhaps the greatest advantage of using the E-2 visa as a path to the EB-5 visa is the length of time the process takes. Presently, it takes the US Embassy in London approximately 15 to 20 days to process the E-2 visa for treaty investors. As previously mentioned, USCIS is currently taking around 16 months to approve EB-5 petitions. Obtaining an approved E-2 visa can significantly reduce the amount of time an investor must remain outside of the United States by over 12 months.

Another advantage is the lower initial investment amount required under the E-2 visa. Unlike the EB-5 visa category, which has a minimum capital investment requirement, the E-2 visa has no such rule. While the regulations state the E-2 investment must be substantial, there is no set dollar amount required. The amount of investment depends on the relevant start-up costs for the individual business.

13

The Importance of a Well-Drafted Business Plan in L1, E2, and EB5 Matters

The United States government expects to see a well-drafted business plan as support for applications in both the E Treaty Visa category and the EB-5 Immigrant Entrepreneur category. Additionally, USCIS often kicks back a request for a "feasibility study" in L1 "New Office" petitions, which is something that is normally included in a well-drafted business plan. Hence, it stands to reason that inclusion of a well-drafted business plan is essential as supporting documentation in an L1 "New Office" Petition.

As evidence of the critical importance of a well-drafted business plan is the fact that the United States government frequently denies L1 visa, E2 visa and EB5 visa petitions and applications due to their lack of a business plan that is both comprehensive and credible.

Business plans that are not comprehensive and are more in the nature of a summary or overview of the business are generally not acceptable for L1 visa, E2 visa, and EB5 visa purposes. Instead, in any one given case the United States government expects to receive and review a business plan that, at minimum:

a. Fully describes the enterprise, its products and services;

b. Analyzes the market in detail, including potential customers and competition;

c. Outlines a marketing strategy;

d. Projects sales, costs, and income over a period of 5 years, <u>showing the basis for these projections</u>; and

e. Presents complete details regarding the enterprises organizational structure, including complete job descriptions and a staffing timetable.

In short, <u>the United States government expects to see a business plan that is as comprehensive as one that would be presented to a bank for purposes of seeking funding.</u> Therefore, it is strongly recommended that one seek the services of a professional who is familiar with the relevant immigration regulations to draft ones business plan if one hopes to stand a strong chance at success in an L1 visa, E2 visa or EB5 visa petition or application.

When selecting the right firm to draft a visa-specific business plan, a company or investor should seek out a firm that possesses both experience in the writing of bespoke business plans as well as the appropriate legal expertise to tailor the plan to the specific requirements of the L1 visa, E2 visa or EB5 visa categories.

To ensure that all the required elements of a well-drafted business plan will be covered to the satisfaction of the United States government, the company or investor should satisfy themselves that all of the following services will be covered by the fee that they will be paying for the business plan writing service:

a. Setup of business plan according to target visa category;

b. Gathering of information and documentation regarding company ownership, objectives and mission;

c. Working with business owner to determine concise statement regarding company's success formula;

d. Work out with owner the visa-appropriate management and staffing plan (i.e., executive/management mix for L1 visa; marginality avoidance for E2 visa; creation of 10 full-time positions over a 2-year period for EB5 visa;

    e. Draft an easy to read service summary;

    f. Collaborate with client to create feasibility study, which covers target market, customer/client potentiality in geographical area (with growth projections), and competition analysis;

    g. Gather financial information to draft financial plan and Tables, including Start-up Summary (as applicable), Sales Forecast, Operating Expenses, and 5-year Projections.

Once the business plan has been developed into its penultimate draft, it should undergo a final review by the responsible immigration attorney to secure an opinion as to the viability of the plan, from a financial perspective. (Obviously, if the responsible immigration attorney is drafting the business plan, his or her opinion will be rendered simultaneously with the creation of the penultimate draft.) Once the responsible immigration attorney has rendered his or her opinion that the plan is fiscally viable, the plan can be finalized and signed off for inclusion in the visa application package.

14

Options Following Denial of a Visa Petition: Administrative Review, Appeals, and Motions

When USCIS denies a visa petition, the law provides strict deadlines in which a motion or an appeal may be filed. You will find the deadline in your particular case at the end of the denial notice.

Failure to file a Motion or Appeal before the specified deadline will result in permanent loss of appeal rights. As such, it is critical that you act straightaway to remedy the denial, to avoid the loss of these important rights.

Depending on the type of Petition you have filed, your immediate remedies may include: Administrative Review; Motion to Reopen; Motion to Reconsider; and Appeal to the AAO or BIA.

It is important to note that only the Petitioner (or their attorney) can file a request for administrative review, a motion or an appeal in a visa petition case. A Beneficiary cannot request administrative review, or file a motion or appeal, unless he is both the Petitioner and the Beneficiary.

I. Administrative Review

Petitioners that paid for Premium Processing may lodge a remedy known as Administrative Review. To succeed in an Administrative Review you will be required to demonstrate that the Reviewing Officer overlooked important evidence or improperly applied the relevant regulations or case law. Success in an Administrative Review may result in a reversal of the Denial. The turnaround time in an Administrative Review is usually 7 to 10 days.

II. Motion to Reopen

A Motion to Reopen is a request to the original decision maker to review a denial. The motion must be based on factual grounds, such as the discovery of new evidence or changed circumstances, and must state the new facts to be considered in the reopened proceedings. A Motion to Reopen may be supported by new affidavits or other documentary evidence.

III. Motion to Reconsider

A Motion to Reconsider is a request to the original decision maker to review a denial, based on legal arguments. The motion must establish that the decision was incorrect based on the evidence on record at the time of the decision, and it must state the reasons for reconsideration. A Motion to Reconsider must be supported by any pertinent precedent decisions to establish that the decision was based on an incorrect application of law or USCIS policy. New evidence or changed circumstances cannot support the filing of a Motion to Reconsider.

A written letter submitted to USCIS is *not considered a motion*. Instead, a motion must be filed on the appropriate form and submitted with the required filing fee, unless the fee is waived.

Generally, motions must be filed within 30 days from the date that USCIS issued its denial — not from the date you actually received the decision in the mail. If you post your motion, you must allow enough time for the document to reach USCIS by the deadline, and make certain that you use recorded delivery to prove that you actually met the deadline.

In most cases, USCIS should issue a written decision on any properly filed motion within 90 days. However, filing a motion will not suspend the execution of any decision made in your case or extend a previously set departure date.

Ultimately, if USCIS denies or dismisses your motion, you may appeal to USCIS Administrative Appeals Office ("AAO") — if the original decision was appealable to the AAO.

IV. Appeals

Generally speaking, an Appeal is a request to a higher authority to review a decision. In a visa petition, the right to Appeal is available only in some unfavorable decisions: either to the AAO or to the Board of Immigration Appeals ("BIA"). Your denial notice will provide information about whether the decision may be appealed, and, if so, whether it should be filed with the AAO or the BIA.

When a petitioner appeals a decision to the AAO, the officer who made the original decision will first review the record. The adjudicating officer will then determine whether the evidence or argument submitted in the appeal warrants reopening or reconsidering the decision. In other words, an appeal to the AAO is also, in effect, a Motion to Reopen or Motion to Reconsider.

If the adjudicating officer determines that reopening or reconsidering the decision is not warranted, she will forward the case for further review to the AAO or the BIA.

As in the case of a Motion to Reopen and a Motion to Reconsider, an appeal generally should be filed within 30 days from the date the decision was issued (not the date you received the decision in the mail). In some cases, a shorter appeal period may apply.

Regardless of the deadline applicable to your case, USCIS does not approve deadline extension requests. Instead, deadlines are strictly enforced. If you fail to file your Appeal in time to meet the deadline, you will forever lose your appeal rights. As in the case of motions, if you post your Appeal, you must allow enough time for the document to reach USCIS by the deadline. A postmark is not enough. Hence, we recommend that you use recorded delivery to prove you actually met the deadline.

V. Appellate Brief

It is not required to submit an appellate brief with an Appeal. However, most well-seasoned appellate lawyers will prepare a forceful appellate brief on behalf of their client, which cites both to the record, as well as to the applicable law, in an effort to have the negative decision overturned.

If you choose to file your own Appeal without the assistance of an appellate lawyer, you must at minimum include a well-written explanation as to why you believe the earlier decision was in error. If you fail to provide either an appellate brief or an explanation of why you believe the decision was in error, your Appeal will likely be denied.

In most cases, the AAO will attempt to decide an appeal within six months of receipt. However, some cases may take longer to decide; especially those in the more complex business categories, such as L-1A and H-1B.

VI. The Importance of Obtaining a Second Opinion

The preparer of the original visa petition is not always the best person to prepare and file a request for Administrative Review, Motion to Reopen, Motion to Reconsider, or Appeal. Instead, it is often recommendable to have ones visa submission reviewed independently in conjunction with the Denial, to allow for maximum objectivity in strategizing a response.

15

US Permanent Residency Through Business Expansion

Multinational business owners and executives are the elite, as far as the US immigration law is concerned. This is why they are classified as having the highest priority when it comes to US Permanent Residency. Their cases are exempted from Labor Certification, and glide through the Green Card process fairly effortlessly, as long as they meet the minimum requirements: At least 1 years employment as an executive (or professional manager) for a company that has an affiliate, subsidiary or parent in *either* the US, or any foreign country.

While the above-mentioned process is fairly obvious and straight-forward in the case of an established ownership arrangement between companies on both sides of the ocean (or, on either side of the border, in the case of Canadian and Mexican entities), it is much less apparent when there is only a foreign company (or companies) and no related US entity. In such a case, the relevant US immigration laws and regulations provide for the following special route to US permanent residency through business expansion:

1. Establishment of a new, qualifying US organization;
2. Transfer of a Director from the foreign company to the new US organization, via an L1 visa, to develop and direct the start-up operations, including the staffing of the organization; and
3. Petition for Permanent Residency for the Director and his or her dependents.

The entire process from initial transfer to US permanent residency status, if properly and expeditiously handled, may take as little as 1.5 years to complete. In the interim, both the foreign company and the US company must continue to trade in earnest.

While the size or the turnover of the foreign company is not directly relevant to the granting of the initial L1 transfer visa, only those businesses or organizations that lend themselves to a corporate structure are likely to be found to be qualifying organizations. This usually rules out retail business and restaurants, unless the parent organization owns and operates multiple units from its corporate offices.

Likewise, while the US subsidiary or affiliate need not mirror the foreign company in its business activities, it must also lend itself to a corporate structure to be considered a qualifying organization. Thus, if a foreign company's goal is to transfer a director to the United States – either temporarily or permanently – we are of the opinion that it should steer clear of retails shops and restaurants.

The ease of the above-specified process has recently led some USCIS Service Centers to raise concerns regarding the bona fides of some of these business expansions, especially those originating outside of Western Europe. These concerns are expressed in the issuance of lengthy Requests for Evidence (RFEs), which request copies of corporate minutes and resolutions, as well as feasibility studies evidencing that the business expansion plan reasonably preceded the initial transfer petition. Thus, it is recommended that one allow no less than 90 days to properly law the groundwork prior to the filing of an expansion petition with USCIS.

16

A New Route to US Residency for Professionals?

T he Administrative Appeals Office (AAO) of US Immigration and Citizenship Service (USCIS) has rendered a decision that potentially opens up another avenue for US permanent residency. This article discusses the decision and explores its implication for similar cases:

In a non-precedent decision, the AAO has rendered a decision that potentially opens up another avenue for US permanent residency. In its decision, the AAO upheld the appeal of an H-1B beneficiary, who had set up a start-up company, and then sponsored himself for an H-1B visa.

As per its usual practice, the Vermont Service Center of USCIS denied the original petition on the grounds that as a start-up company without employees the petitioner did not establish that it had sufficient H-1B caliber work to keep the beneficiary employed on a full time basis for three years. USCIS also asserted that as a one-person business, the beneficiary would be responsible for administrative and clerical duties, which are not H-1B qualifying duties. Finally, USCIS stated that the beneficiary could not assume his role without having clientele established, work contracts in place, and expectations of the proffered position defined.

In its decision overturning USCIS denial, the AAO found that the petitioner, an LLC established under the laws of New York, qualified as a US employer under the relevant Federal regulations. Thus, as a separate legal entity from the beneficiary, the petitioner had the legal capacity to submit an offer of employment to the beneficiary, and the beneficiary would not be "self-employed", despite the fact that he would be the company's sole employee. Additionally, the AAO cited a prior decision (*Matter of Aphrodite*, 17 I&N Dec. 520, 1980) and agreed with its ruling that a petitioner's sole owner could be the same person as the sole beneficiary.

In the words of the AAO, "[e]stablished tenets of corporate law, as well as cases such as *Matter of Aphrodite*, state that a corporation has a separate legal identity from its own. As such, a corporation, even if it is owned and operated by a single person, may hire that same individual and the parties will be in an employer-employee relationship, as is the case in the instant matter".

In the opinion of the author, this decision opens the door to another potential avenue to permanent residency in the United States, in that a professional without a job offer could literally form a corporation or LLC in the United States, secure premises for his company, extend an offer of employment to himself, and then petition for an H-1B visa. Securing H-1B status, which can last up to 6 years, could be used as a stepping stone to permanent residency in either one of two ways:

1. The H1 professional's own company could apply for Labor Certification and then petition for permanent residency for the professional; or

2. The H1 professional could shift his visa to another company using AC21 Portability, and then rely on the sponsorship of the new employer.

Of course, as in all H-1B visa cases, this strategy will be subject to the H-1B visa cap, and will depend on the occupational classification of the proffered position, the educational credentials of the professional, and the ability of the company to pay the prevailing wage for the position. All of these considerations must be carefully considered and, preferably, guided by an experienced business immigration lawyer to avoid any missteps.

Arguably, this strategy is less favorable than that offered by acquisition of L1A status in the United States, in that it does not lead to fast-track residency after one year. However, it certainly has the advantage of not requiring ownership or employment in a foreign business, it does not require continued operation of a foreign business, and it does not require that the visa holder exercise strictly executive-level duties.

In any case, this strategy is definitely superior to the E2 visa, in that the H-1B visa category is a dual intent category that allows one to pursue permanent residency without fear of having one's status invalidated. Furthermore, H-1B visa status is not reserved for nationals of certain countries, as is the E2 visa, and does not require application through the United States Embassy or Consulate abroad.

In summary, professionals contemplating a permanent move to the United States now have another potential avenue for realizing their goal, that does not rely on ownership of a foreign business, investment of a substantial sum of cash in advance of visa approval, or obtaining a job offer. Of course, this strategy is not for everyone. One must hold the appropriate university degree, have the resources to launch a formal office, and one must have the courage to make ones own way.

17

Demystifying the H2B Visa

The H-2B is a little understood temporary employment-based visa. Employers are often confused by the concept of *temporary need*, as defined by the relevant regulations, and face the daunting task of proving the unavailability of local labor. In the case of the construction industry, the task is made more difficult by union interference. This article attempts to clarify the H-2B requirements for employers, and makes general recommendations.

It happens all the time these days. A contractor is awarded a large contract, but finds he doesn't have enough workers to perform the job. He advertises the position, asks around the community, always with the same result - no workers available. Finally, as a last resort, he considers importing qualified skilled workers from outside the United States, but everyone tells him it is legally impossible to import such workers. So he ends up violating the law by hiring undocumented workers, as a matter of survival. Something is wrong with this picture.

What is wrong with the picture is the misperception that importing skilled workers is legally impossible. This misperception has been perpetuated over the years by the likes of the US Department of Labor and even, more surprisingly, by over-cautious immigration lawyers.

It is a misperception that has so worked its way into the very psyche of the construction industry and the legal community, that there have been calls on Capitol Hill for immigration reform and for new treaties between the US and Mexico to address the labor shortage problem. In fact, before the tragedy of September 11th, 2001, President George Bush was in the midst of holding high-level meetings with Mexican President Vicente Fox on the subject. These talks have since come to a halt, like many other exigencies, in the interests of Homeland Security.

Unfortunately, a lot of time and effort has been wasted trying to fix the labor shortage problem, and all the hysterics and calls for immigration reform have been for the most part unnecessary. The truth is that there is actually a little-used provision in the immigration law for importation of temporary skilled labor: the much-misunderstood "H-2B visa." This goal of this article is to demystify and clarify exactly what the H-2B visa is all about, and to offer some general information as to how a contractor might go about obtaining approval from the government for the temporary importation of workers from offshore.

I. Obtaining a Temporary Labor Certification

A contractor who seeks to import skilled labor for his short-term needs must first obtain a *Labor Certificate* for a specified number of workers from the US Department of Labor (DOL). He does this by presenting evidence to the DOL that his need for labor is temporary and that there are no workers available in the local labor market. Once the contractor has obtained the *Labor Certificate*, he files this with US Citizenship and Immigration Services (USCIS), which then authorizes the visas. USCIS will deny any visa request that does not include a *Labor Certificate*.

II. Temporary Need Defined

A temporary need is defined in the applicable laws and regulations as a need that is less than twelve months. Additionally, the need must fall into one of the following categories: one-time need, seasonal need, peak-load need, or intermittent need. In the construction industry, the category that is most often used is the peak load need, which usually recurs annually. In any case, the contractor must present documentary evidence of his temporary need along with the application for Temporary Labor Certificate. Failure to provide such documentation is always fatal to a case. Other documents that are helpful in establishing a temporary need are a detailed itinerary and any larger than normal contracts.

III. Proving the Unavailability of Local Workers

Proving that there are no available workers in the local labor pool involves advertising the position in a local newspaper of general circulation for three consecutive days. The DOL also opens a job order on the internet for a period of ten days. Interested applicants are instructed to send their resumes and references directly to the DOL, which then forwards these to the contractor. Given the current labor shortage, our experience has been that few, if any, qualified workers send their resumes to the DOL. Those that do rarely show up for work if offered a job. In any event, the contractor must contact any applicant that appears to meet the minimum qualifications. Once the recruitment period comes to an end (usually 14 days), the contractor send a statement of recruitment results to the DOL and waits two or three weeks for approval of the Labor Certificate.

IV. Union Involvement

An extra-congressional, internal DOL policy singles out the construction industry as having to get union clearance before the DOL will issue a Temporary Labor Certificate. It is our opinion that this is a burdensome and discriminatory policy. At present, we are informed that a preliminary understanding with DOL officials in Washington D.C. and in Boston has been reached that notification of the appropriate union local is sufficient, so long as the contractor proves that the contact was made. If the union then wishes to refer individuals, they must apply as individuals through the normal channels. The union may not simply send over a roster of names. Additionally, the union has only 5 days in which to make its referrals. This understanding, as stated above, is only preliminary. Total elimination of the union notification requirement is preferred by non-shop contractors seeking to employ alien labor.

V. Room for Expansion

There are currently 66,000 H-2B visas available every year. However, on average, only 40,000 visas are actually utilized in any one year. This is in marked contrast to the better known H-1B visa, which is utilized to import professional labor. The H-1B visa was originally capped out at 65,000 visa per year, and each year there were more visa applications than available visas. At the insistence of the High Tech and IT lobby, congress raised the cap in excess of 200,000 visas per year. Although the number of available H-1B visas is back down to 65,000, the precedent for the solution is established nonetheless: Even if contractors suddenly take advantage of the H-2B visa to address their temporary labor needs (as the IT industry has done), there is no problem if the visa demand exceeds the supply of available visas - congress can always raise the cap as it has done before.

VI. A Win-Win Situation

Contractors that take advantage of the H-2B visa to solve their short-term labor needs will not only benefit themselves, but will benefit the labor market on the whole. They will not need to continually run afoul of the law by hiring undocumented workers. Instead, they can bring these same workers into the system (regardless of whether they come from Mexico or Canada or Europe), use their valuable services for several months each year, and then let them go home for a few months until the next peak-load or seasonal labor cycle. At the same time, these same contractors will have effectively solved their short-term labor problems and will no longer have to turn down or lose valuable contracts due to lack of workers. In the meantime, the United States construction industry will have the time to find local solutions to the skilled labor shortage.

18

Determining Eligibility for US Immigration Benefits for a Dependent Spouse or Partner

oving to a new country is one of life's biggest events. Whether one is relocating to take up a temporary work assignment, or permanently immigrating, one's spouse (or life partner) is normally essential to the equation and will often play a vital supporting role in the process. It is, therefore, essential to ensure in advance that the immigration laws of the country in question recognize this important individual as a proper "spouse" for immigration or visa purposes.

The United States currently takes a narrow view on the definition of a *spouse* for immigration purposes. The result of this is that spouses and partners in many not-uncommon types of marriages and relationships are entitled only to limited − if any − immigration benefits. In this article, we review the criteria used by the United States government to determine whether it will recognize a *spouse* for immigration purposes, as well as how said criteria applies to several marital situations.

I. The Three-Prong Test:

United States Citizenship and Immigration Services ("USCIS") and the United States Department of State ("DOS") both apply a three-prong test to assess the validity of a marriage for immigration purposes. The following three-prong test is applied both in assessing eligibility for a derivative non-immigrant visa (e.g., L2 visa, E2 visa, H4 visa, etc.) or an immigrant visa, as well as in matters of family-based sponsorship by a United States Citizen or Legal Permanent Resident:

Prong 1: Was the marriage valid in the place of celebration?

USCIS and DOS both judge the validity of the marriage based on the laws of the place where the marriage was celebrated. A marriage that is not valid in the place where it was celebrated will not be recognized as a marriage for the purposes of receiving immigration benefits.

By way of example, a marriage in Thailand must be registered with the civil registrar, the Amphur. A religious ceremony alone does not create a valid marriage in Thailand. Thus, although a religious ceremony may be sufficient to register a marriage in certain states in the United States, if the marriage that took place in Thailand was only a religious ceremony, without the required civil registration, the spouse will not be eligible for United States immigration benefits due to the invalidity of the marriage in Thailand.

By contrast, informal and tribal ceremonies that would not rise to the formality normally required to register a marriage in the United States may qualify for immigration benefits if the ceremonies meet all of the legal requirements to be valid in the country performed. This element comes up often with common law marriages, which are discussed later in further detail.

There may be the opportunity to cure an invalid marriage and obtain immigration benefits. In an opinion by the General Counsel for the former Immigration and Nationality Service, now USCIS, an Iranian mosque marriage that was performed in Turkey was found not to be valid under the laws of Turkey; however, a subsequent civil marriage validated the marriage in Turkey, thus rendering the spouse eligible for immigration benefits. (See *INS General Counsel Legal Opinion No.*

91–58, File No. CO831 (July 25, 1991)). Marriages that were previously ineligible for United States immigration benefits may even be cured by subsequent laws in the relevant country that cause the previously defective marriages to be recognized as valid in that country.

This approach also applies in determining whether a prior divorce was valid; USCIS and DOS will look to whether the subsequent remarriage was considered valid in the jurisdiction where it took place.

Prong 2: Is there a strong public policy against this type of marriage in the state of domicile or, for couples who marry abroad, the state of intended domicile?

USCIS and DOS may refuse to recognize a spouse for purposes of immigration benefits in some exceptional circumstances when the marriage is contrary to public health or morals, including plural marriages and marriages between close relatives. Each of these situations requires complex analysis and is discussed later in further detail.

Prong 3: Is the marriage bona fide *as defined by immigration law?*

The United States Congress may prescribe a federal standard under which certain marriages, although valid at the place of celebration, are not recognized for immigration benefits. Such federal standards also disregard and override any public policy in favor or against such marriages in the state of current or intended domicile.

The most notable of such Congressional standards is the 1996 Defense of Marriage Act (DOMA), which defines marriage as the legal union between one man and one woman. Under DOMA, applications for immigration benefits based on a marriage of two persons of the same-sex have been uniformly denied, regardless of whether the marriage was entered into in a country that legally recognizes same-sex marriages. DOMA also supersedes any state law in regards to immigration benefits and restricts immigration benefits regardless of whether the same-sex couple will be living in a US state that recognizes same-sex marriage. Visa options for same-sex partners and spouses are discussed later in further detail.

Immigration laws also prescribe that proxy marriages or marriages for the sole purpose of obtaining immigration benefits ("sham marriages") are not recognized as bona fide marriages. A proxy marriage involves a ceremony where the marrying individuals are not in each other's physical presence, but rather are married by picture, telephone, radio, television, or similar. Such marriages may not entitle the spouse to immigration benefits even if it is considered a valid marriage in the place of performance. However, proxy marriages may lead to immigration benefits if it can be shown that the couple consummated the marriage through cohabitation following the ceremony, thus resulting in a bona fide marriage under US immigration laws.

A marriage that is entered into by parties without the intention to live as man and wife, but rather to obtain immigration benefits, will not be considered a bona fide marriage for the purpose of obtaining such benefit regardless of being otherwise valid. Such sham marriages not only prevent the foreign spouse from obtaining immigration benefits, but in cases where a United States Citizen or Legal Permanent Resident files an immigrant petition based on a sham marriage, the United States Citizen or Legal Permanent Resident may face criminal sanctions including imprisonment and fines.

The main consideration by USCIS when evaluating a potential sham marriage is whether the parties intended to establish a life together at the time of the marriage. USCIS looks to the conduct of the parties for this determination, including evidence of courtship, the circumstances of the wedding ceremony, shared residences, insurance policies, bank accounts, and property agreements. Other factors often considered include large age differences, language barriers, and other religious and cultural differences.

USCIS does not, however, consider the following factors to be automatically indicative of a sham marriage if the marriage is otherwise valid and subsisting: 1.) Cohabitation of the parties to the marriage, but without sexual relations because of age or illness; or, 2.) The legal or physical separation of the parties, without dissolution of the marriage. A separated spouse may still be entitled to immigration benefits if there exists an intention to reconcile.

II. The Three-Prong Test in Practice

Looking now to the application of the three-prong test, following is an examination of current USCIS and DOS policy on immigration benefits for same-sex couples, transgender spouses, cohabitating partners and common law spouses, plural marriages, and incestuous marriages:

a. Same-Sex Couples [OUT OF DATE]

USCIS and DOS will deny an application for immigration benefits as a spouse in a same-sex marriage or civil partnership based on the Defense of Marriage Act (DOMA), as of the date of this article.

Section 3 of DOMA states in relevant part that:

In determining the meaning of any Act of Congress, or of any ruling, regulation, or interpretation of the various administrative bureaus and agencies of the United States, the word 'marriage' means only a legal union between one man and one woman as husband and wife, and the word 'spouse' refers only to a person of the opposite sex who is a husband or a wife.

In February 2011, Attorney General Eric Holder announced that the Obama Administration had determined that Section 3 of DOMA was unconstitutional and that the Department of Justice would no longer defend it in federal court challenges. However, the Department of Justice must still enforce DOMA pending a legislative repeal of the act or similar final judicial decision. Numerous and significant court cases are currently ongoing regarding this issue, while a number of legislative acts have also been introduced to the United States Congress. However, at the time of this article, DOMA remains controlling.

Based on DOMA, USCIS and DOS stand firm that any derivative visa, immigrant sponsorship, cancellation of removal, fiancé(e) visas, or waiver application dependent upon a *spousal* relationship, filed based on a same-sex-marriage or civil partnership, will be denied. Furthermore, USCIS and DOS will make an immediate decision on such matters, per standard processing times. USCIS and DOS will not honor requests that USCIS and DOS hold filed cases until the resolution of DOMA litigation.

A same-sex spouse must therefore seek alternative visa options to accompany a spouse holding a non-immigrant visa or to join his or her United States Citizen or Legal Permanent Resident spouse in the United States.

A subsection of the B-2 visitor visa provisions authorize DOS to issue special visitor visas to the same-sex spouse or partner of a foreign national that holds a long-term non-immigrant visa. This type of visitor visa contains a particular annotation that the holder is the same-sex spouse or partner to ease questioning and scrutiny by officers at the port of entry to the United States. However, like ordinary visitor visas, the same-sex spouse or partner will only be given authorized entry to the United States of up to six (6) months at a time. Stays for longer than six (6) months will need to be authorized by filing applications to extend status in the United States, with the associated fees. Furthermore, the same-sex spouse or partner is not authorized to work in the United States, whether or not the work is paid, and regardless of whether the work is for a United States company or foreign company. If the same-sex spouse or partner wishes to work in the United States, he or she will need to obtain an appropriate visa in his or her own right.

This subsection of the visitor visa regulations does not apply to the same-sex spouses or partners of United States Citizens or Legal Permanent Residents. In adjudicating all visitor visa applications, DOS must determine that the applicant's visit is temporary and that the applicant has significant ties to their home country. A marriage to a United States Citizen or Legal Permanent Resident residing in the United States, even when the marriage is not recognized by United States immigration laws, may result in the denial of a visitor visa application by DOS based on the presumption by DOS that the applicant will not return to their home country, but will rather remain in the United States with their spouse or partner.

Same-sex spouses or partners of United States Citizens and Legal Permanent Residents will need to obtain an appropriate visa in their own right. Some of the options to do so could include investing in a business in the United States, a transfer from a foreign employer to an affiliated United States employer, finding United States employment sponsorship, or enrolling in an approved education or training course. Each of these options needs to be fully evaluated against the qualifications and circumstances of the same-sex spouse.

b. Transsexual Marriage

A marriage in which the two parties were born the same-sex, but where one party underwent gender reassignment surgery, may entitle the spouse to immigration benefits. The Board of Immigration Appeals held in the *Matter of Lovo-Lara* that DOMA did not apply to transsexuals in a heterosexual relationship based on post-operative gender. Therefore, the analysis of whether the marriage is recognized turns back to the validity in the jurisdiction of the marriage.

The controlling test in determining whether such marriages are recognized for immigration purposes is whether the marriage was considered a valid and heterosexual marriage in the jurisdiction where the marriage occurred. The marriage in the precedent case of *Matter of Lovo-Lara*, as an example, occurred in the state of North Carolina. The transsexual spouse obtained a permitted change of the sex on her birth certificate following her gender reassignment to female and then married her male husband. The court noted that North Carolina registered their marriage as legal, but that same-sex marriage is not legal in North Carolina. Thus, the marriage was both considered heterosexual and valid in North Carolina, and the spouse was entitled to immigration benefits.

A number of US states, as well as foreign countries, have legal precedent as to whether such a marriage is valid and heterosexual in that jurisdiction. In reviewing whether the marriage is valid and heterosexual, it is important to note that some jurisdictions, including Illinois and Texas, allow a post-operative transsexual to change the gender on their birth certificate, but do not recognize the gender reassignment as changing the individual's sex for purposes of marriages. Also, a marriage in which one party is a post-operative transsexual may be recognized in some jurisdictions as a valid marriage, but still as a same-sex marriage. The registered same-sex marriage would not recognized for immigration purposes per DOMA.

In many jurisdictions the statute is not clear or there is no binding precedent. In such case, USCIS may be satisfied as to the validity of the marriage through submission of a court order, official record, or statement from an appropriate government agency indicating that the gender reassignment surgery has resulted in a change of the person's legal sex under the law of the place of the marriage.

Accordingly, the marriage of two parties who were born the same-sex may be recognized for immigration benefits if all of the following are satisfied:

i.) One individual underwent gender reassignment surgery; *and*

ii.) The person who underwent gender reassignment surgery has taken whatever legal steps exist and may be required to have the legal change of sex recognized for purposes of marriage under the law of the place of marriage; *and*

iii.) The marriage is recognized under the law of the jurisdiction of marriage as a valid and heterosexual marriage.

c. Common Law Marriages

An actual marriage between two people made *without formal registry*, often known as a *common law marriage*, is recognized for purposes of immigration benefits only if common law marriages are recognized in the jurisdiction where the unregistered marriage took place. In reviewing the validity of these marriages, USCIS and DOS will look first to determine if *common law marriages* were recognized by the jurisdiction at the time of unregistered marriage, and then as to whether the parties fulfilled all of the requirements of the jurisdiction to create a common law marriage, such as mutual agreement, cohabitation, etc.

USCIS and DOS will also look to ensure that the recognition of the common law marriage by the jurisdiction bestows all of the same legal rights and duties as individuals in lawfully contracted marriages. Factors for consideration include, but are not limited to, whether the relationship can only be terminated by divorce and if there is an intestate distribution of an estate.

Most US states no longer recognize common law marriages. However, unless the jurisdiction has invalidated common law marriages recognized under former regulations, USCIS and DOS will rely on whether the common law marriage was recognized at the time of its inception, regardless of whether the jurisdiction is currently recognizing new common law marriages.

d. Cohabitating Partners

Cohabitating partners who have not entered into a valid, registered marriage and are not in a recognized common law marriage are not eligible for the immigration benefits of a spouse. Similar to same-sex partners, heterosexual partners cohabitating in a relationship akin to marriage are eligible to apply for a special visitor visa to accompany a partner travelling to the United States with a long-term non-immigrant visa. This special visitor visa authorizes entry to the United States for up to six (6) months, with extensions of up to six (6) months at a time possible from within the United States upon further application to USCIS. If the cohabitating partner wishes to work in the United States, he or she will need to obtain the appropriate United States visa in his or her own right.

It is unlikely that DOS will issue a cohabitating partner of a United States Citizen or Legal Permanent Resident a visitor visa if the United States Citizen or Legal Permanent Resident is living in the United States, due to the presumption that the partner will not return to their foreign residency. Cohabitating partners in these situations will either need to obtain an appropriate long-term non-immigrant visa or enter into a valid marriage to obtain immigration benefits.

e. Plural (Polygamous) Marriages

United States law does not recognize plural (i.e. "polygamous") marriages, regardless of whether the marriages in question are legal and recognized in the jurisdiction of marriages. Thus, a marriage that is entered into before a previous marriage of either party is ended by divorce, annulment or death is void and invalid for US immigration purposes. (Note: Disappearance of one spouse may also constitute the legal end of a marriage in certain jurisdictions.)

In cases where the soundness of the divorce is in question, USCIS and DOS look to whether the first marriage was fully and legally terminated based on the law of the jurisdiction of the termination and whether the second marriage was regarded as lawful at its place of celebration, as a monogamous marriage. For example, in *Matter of Moncayo*, the Board of Immigration Appeals found that a divorce decree that was issued in Ecuador in the absence of one party to the divorce was not valid in New York, thus the party's remarriage in New York was not valid.

Even when the intent is for a monogamous marriage, individuals seeking immigration benefits as, or for, a spouse that has entered into a previous marriage should ensure that the prior marriage was properly terminated. If the prior marriage was not properly terminated and the current marriage is void, the beneficiary/spouse will not be eligible for immigration benefits until the prior marriage is properly terminated and a valid marriage occurs.

Whilst polygamy is legal and practiced in many customs and cultures around the world, it is illegal in the United States and immigration law recognizes only the first of the plural marriages. The discussion of immigration benefits in such marriages will be discussed from the perspective of one husband with plural wives; however, the discussion applies identically to a situation of one wife with plural husbands.

Only the first wife of a polygamist husband who obtains a long-term non-immigrant visa to the United States, such as the L-1 visa, may obtain a derivative non-immigrant visa, such as the L-2 visa. It is not simply that only one wife may accompany the polygamist husband, it is that only his first wife is eligible for a derivative visa as the marriages to later wives are void and invalid under United States immigration law.

The second wife and any later wives will need to qualify for a long-term non-immigrant visa in their own right, as the principal applicant, to able to accompany their husband to the United States on a long-term basis. DOS also grants officers at United States Embassies and Consulates the discretion to issue visitor visas to plural wives to accompany their husband.

While the husband and the first wife are eligible for non-immigrant visas, the Immigration and Nationality Act § 212(a)(10)(A) renders polygamists ineligible for immigrant visas. This section only renders individuals that practice polygamy inadmissible and it does not extend to individuals who merely believe in or advocate polygamy without themselves entering into plural marriages. A polygamist that wishes to become a Legal Permanent Resident of the United States will need to divorce all wives besides his first and abandon the practice of polygamy before commencing the residency process. DOS consular officers are instructed to be suspicious of former polygamists who divorce plural wives just before moving forward with the residency process and must review the matter to ensure that the former polygamist will not resume the practice following issuance of Legal Permanent Resident status.

f. Incestuous Marriages

An incestuous marriage between close relatives will only be recognized for immigration benefits if the marriage was valid at the place of origin *and* the cohabitation of the parties at their intended residence in the United States will not incur criminal punishment. When looking at the factor of the intended residence, the controlling factor is not whether the state performs such marriages, but rather if the state deems such marriages or relationships illegal. Marriages by cousins and by an uncle and niece are not illegal in many states and have led to immigration benefits.

Conclusion

All of the above-discussed situations create complex and often challenging immigration cases that must be handled with care. USCIS and DOS do not offer guidance or specific instructions on the appropriate presentation of these cases, nor should it be assumed that USCIS and DOS are fully practiced in such situations. The guidance of immigration lawyers who are well-versed in such cases will help to ensure that the appropriate visa category is sought and that the legal eligibility for the immigration benefit, with appropriate documentation, is thoroughly demonstrated to USCIS and DOS for the most efficient processing.

19

The American Dream: Introduction to the EB5 Immigrant Investor Visa

The American Dream is alive and well, and people across the world are fulfilling their own US immigration goals via the EB-5 Visa Program. Compared with other countries, the United States is still a safe place to invest money, raise a family and start a business. The EB-5 visa allows immigrant investors to live and work permanently anywhere in the country. The visa even includes passive investment opportunities for those who do not wish to work, or would prefer to work someplace other than the EB-5 project they invested in.

The United States' foundation was built by immigrant communities, and despite economic hardship across the globe, people still flock to the US for new opportunities.

The EB-5 visa allows a foreign national the opportunity to make a qualified investment into a US business in exchange for a green card for themselves and certain family members. Unlike other US visa categories, the EB-5 visa does not require a job offer, educational credentials, English language skill or family sponsorship. Provided the immigrant investor invests the requisite funds and meets additional requirements, they will qualify for a green card.

The EB-5 visa was created by the US Congress to stimulate the economy through job creation. The program requires an investment of $1,000,000 USD, which would create or save at least 10 US jobs. The investment may be reduced to $500,000 USD for businesses located in a Target Employment Area ("TEA"). An area may qualify as a TEA if it is suffering from high unemployment or is classified as a rural area.

Potential immigrant investors can choose between making a Direct EB-5 Investment through creation of their own business. They will be responsible for managing the day-to-day activities of the business, as well as meeting the job creation requirements. Alternatively, an investor wishing to take a more passive role in their investment can choose the Indirect Regional Centre investment path. Regional Centres are approved by USCIS to operate EB-5 projects within their designated boundaries. Most Regional Centre investments are located in a TEA and qualify for the reduced $500,000 USD investment. Further, a Regional Centre investment allows for the counting of indirect job to satisfy the job creation requirements.

Along with a properly submitted EB-5 petition, the immigrant investor should be able to trace their investment funds to a lawful source. Accordingly, documentation and evidence for how the investor obtained his/her investment funds should be provided to the filing attorney.

A successful EB-5 petition will provide the investor a two-year conditional green card. Following the conditional green card, the immigrant investor will need to prove to USCIS that all the conditions of the EB-5 visa were met, at which time, he or she will receive a ten-year renewable green card.

20

Myths Associates with the EB5 Immigrant Investor Visa

As a full-service EB-5 immigration law firm, we frequently receive enquiries from prospective immigrant investors who have been misinformed regarding the EB-5 program requirements and eligibility. Unfortunately, the misinformation they receive often comes from retaining an inexperienced EB-5 immigration lawyer or consulting with an unlicensed migration agent. Some of the most common EB-5 myths we hear can be found below.

Myth 1: "I own a residential property in the United States valued at over $1,000,000 USD. Therefore, I qualify to apply for an EB-5 visa and US permanent residency."

The Reality: Simply owning a residential property in the United States valued at over $1,000,000 USD does not allow a potential immigrant investor to qualify for the EB-5 visa. The qualified invested capital must be made in a new commercial enterprise which has the capacity to support ten full-time jobs for qualified employees.

Myth 2: "I'm not eligible to apply for the EB-5 visa because I do not have a university degree and do not speak English very well."

The Reality: Provided the investor meets the minimum investment amount and submits evidence that their funds were lawfully obtained, they may apply for the EB-5 visa program. There is no education, English language, job offer, or family sponsorship requirement to apply. This is one aspect that makes the EB-5 Immigrant Investor Visa so appealing.

Myth 3: "I found an EB-5 project that will guarantee my invested capital. Therefore, I'm more likely to have my EB-5 petition approved."

The Reality: The immigration rules and regulations do not allow for the EB-5 investment to be guaranteed. The investment must be considered to be "at risk" for immigration purposes. Any guarantee of returning the investment capital will be grounds for denial of the EB-5 petition. That said, our firm only works with reputable EB-5 projects with a track record of immigration success.

Myth 4: "I am unfamiliar with US business practices and do not feel comfortable running a business in the United States. I certainly would not be able to meet the 10 job creation requirement for the EB-5 visa. Therefore, I am ineligible to apply through the EB-5 program for permanent residency."

The Reality: For potential immigrant investors not comfortable establishing their own business and meeting the EB-5 job requirements, there is a passive EB-5 investment option they may choose. Projects located within a USCIS approved Regional Centres are designated to pool investor's funds and actively manage the EB-5 project without requiring the investor's participation. The immigrant investor may choose to live or work anywhere in the United States, regardless of where their investment is located.

Myth 5: "The EB-5 visa is just a way for wealthy foreign nationals to buy a green card. It serves no benefit to the United States."

The Reality: EB-5 investors contribute to the promotion and success of the US economy. Each individual's capital investment is required by law, to create ten full-time jobs for US citizens or other immigrants authorized to work in the United States. Along with job creation,

EB-5 investors stimulate the economy through the purchase of homes, vehicles, and other consumer products. The EB-5 visa program has contributed greatly to the US economy since its creation in 1990.

Myth 6: "I can't apply for the EB-5 visa because I did not personally earn the money to make the investment – it was given to me as a gift."

The Reality: Most lawfully earned funds can be used for the EB-5 capital investment. This can include an irrevocable gift, or any a loan secured on the personal assets of the investor. The important aspect of EB-5 funding is that the money can be traced back to a lawful source. Funds earned through criminal activity may not be used to obtain an EB-5 visa.

Myth 7: "I'm currently in the United States on a tourist visa. Therefore, I can remain in the US while my EB-5 petition is pending with USCIS, and file for adjustment of status once it is approved."

The Reality: Unfortunately, this would not be possible. One is only eligible for adjustment of status in the United States if they maintain an eligible non-immigrant status through the time when the EB-5 visa is approved. The current processing time for an I-526 petition (EB-5 visa) is over 12 months. A tourist visa does not allow its holder to remain in the United States for more than six months out of every calendar year.

Myth 8: "I do not qualify for an EB-5 visa because I do not have $1,000,000 USD to invest."

The Reality: When the EB-5 Immigrant Investor Visa program was originally introduced in 1990, the $1,000,000 USD investment was the only option. However, in 1992, Congress enacted the Regional Centre Pilot Program, which authorized a reduced investment of $500,000 USD for investments made in Targeted Employment Area ("TEA"). TEAs are rural areas with a population of less than 20,000, and locations suffering from high unemployment of at least 150% of the national average.

Myth 9: "I have invested over $1,000,000 USD in a new commercial enterprise located within the United States. However, I only have a 25%

ownership interest of the business. Therefore, I am not able to apply for an EB-5 visa."

The Reality: There is no set ownership requirement in order to qualify for the EB-5 visa. An immigrant investor need only meet the minimum investment amount, along with the other relevant immigration requirements. A potential investor could own 1% or 100% of the business and still qualify if all other requirements are met.

Myth 10: "I do not believe the United States has a treaty of commerce and navigation with my country of nationality. Therefore, I am ineligible to obtain permanent residency through the EB-5 visa program."

The Reality: Do not confuse the EB-5 Immigrant Investor Visa with the E-2 Treaty Investor Visa. Unlike the E-2 visa, there is no nationality, ownership interest, or residency requirement to be eligible for the EB-5 visa. A treaty of commerce and navigation is not necessary for you apply for the visa.

Conclusion

These are just a handful of the EB-5 visa myths that are promoted through the internet, or by an unlicensed "migration" agent. Potential investors who rely on these myths, or the public domain for their information may suffer serious immigration consequences, including the denial of an EB-5 petition and loss of invested capital.

21

Cost of an EB5 Regional Center Investment

As an immigration attorney representing EB-5 investors, one of the frequently asked questions is: *What is the total cost of an EB-5 Regional Center investment?* Savvy investors understand, in order to go through the EB-5 Visa process, they will incur expenses *additional to* the $500,000 capital investment.

So what is the cost of an EB-5 investment? Unfortunately, there is no set dollar amount. Each investor's case is distinct, and there are a multitude of factors that may influence the associated costs. This article addresses the most common EB-5 costs. However, it is quite important to bear in mind that expenditures for each specific case may vary.

I. The Investment

One cost that is universal for all clients is the *invested capital.* Most Regional Center projects are located in a Targeted Employment Area ("TEA"), which allows for a reduced investment amount of $500,000.

II. Legal Fees

Just as one would not forgo obtaining a specialist surgeon to perform a delicate operation, one should also likewise retain a competent EB-5 attorney to file ones Green Card petition. Depending on whether ones lawyer bills a flat fee or hourly rate for an EB-5 investment, one may expect to pay anywhere from $10,000 to $25,000 for the relevant, specialized legal services. Depending on the firm one chooses, this fee may or may not include the services of an EB-5 Investment Advisor.

III. Project Administration Fees

The majority of projects out there charge an administration fee when subscribing to their project. The typical administration fee ranges from $30,000 to $60,000. These fees are generally used to pay marketing costs, as well as *finder fees* for agents abroad.

IV. Government Filing Fees

With every I-526 Petition filed, USCIS requires the payment of a filing fee. Currently, the filing fee for an I-526 Petition is $1,500.

V. Translation Fees

USCIS requires any documentation or evidence not written in the English language to be accompanied by an English language translation. Further, at a recent EB-5 stakeholder meeting, USCIS indicated that the entire subject document must be translated, and abstract translations are not acceptable. Translation service fees vary depending on the document content and number of words. One may expect to pay between $0.25 and $0.50 per word.

VI. Miscellaneous Costs

If one chooses to travel to the US to meet with Regional Center representative or with ones attorney, one is likely to incur additional expenses such as travel, housing and visa costs.

Although these are a few of the most common expenses associated with the EB-5 investor visa, additional costs may arise depending on ones individual case. One may also be able to mitigate the costs of EB-5 through various means. That said, a conservative estimate of a typical EB-5 investment and associated costs—from start to finish—will be approximately $600,000.

22

EB5 Regional Centers & Securities Law

EB-5 investors are becoming increasingly aware of the Securities and Exchange Commission (SEC), the top US securities regulator, and its involvement in the EB-5 Visa Program. As a result, investors are anxious to learn the connection between the nation's financial watchdog and the immigration program.

Created by the Securities Act of 1934, the SEC was designed to protect investors from fraud by enforcing securities laws requiring complete disclosure of information and regulating the people involved in the securities transactions. Attorneys handling EB-5 Visa clients should be prepared to provide a competent explanation on both immigration and securities issues involved in the EB-5 process.

In the past, securities law was considered a specialty area of law reserved for large firms in cities such as New York. However, at present, to practice as an EB-5 attorney, it is important to have at least a minimum understanding of the US securities law.

The SEC defines a security as any stock, bond, debenture, note, transferable share, investment contract or certificate of interest in a profit-sharing agreement. In general, all securities offered in the United States must be registered with the SEC and comply with the regulations, or be eligible to claim an exemption from registration. A typical EB-5 Regional Center Project is structured in the form of a Limited Partnership and according to SEC, interest in the partnership is an investment contract and therefore, a security.

To further elaborate on the term *investment contract*, the Supreme Court of the United States determined the definition in the landmark case of *SEC v. Howey*. According to the Supreme Court, as per *Howey*, an investment contract is any transaction in which: (1) a person invests money (2) in a common enterprise (3) is led to expect profits and (4) solely from the efforts of others. These four elements combined are commonly referred to as the *Howey Test* and are used to determine whether an instrument qualifies an investment contract.

The first element is interpreted as the investor not purchasing a consumable commodity or service, rather, making an actual bona fide at risk investment. The second element of commonality is determined by multiple investors having interrelated interest in a common scheme (it is sufficient if a single investor has a common interest). The third element of expectation of profits is interpreted as expected returns must come from the earnings of the enterprise. Lastly, earnings must come from the efforts of others, this is broadly construed to mean that the efforts of managers must predominate over the passive investor.

EB-5 Regional Center Projects structured as a Limited Partnership meet all 4 elements of the *Howey Test* and are therefore defined as an *investment contract*. Foreign investors (1) invest at minimum $500,000 (2) into a common enterprise, Limited Partnership, (3) with an expectation of returns on the investment and (4) through the efforts of the managing partner.

Simply meeting the definition of a security is just the beginning of the complex regulations of US securities.

23

Mandatory Reporting of Foreign Investment in the United States

The relative strength of the British Pound against the US Dollar recently has led a large number of Brits to liquidate their assets in Britain and relocate to the balmy climes of such US states as Florida and California. Some have chosen to make the move as *investors* via the E2 Treaty Investor visa program. Others have made the move by establishing US subsidiaries of their UK companies and transferring themselves to the US as L-1A multinational executives.

Most of these individuals will make the required investments or acquisitions completely ignorant of the US law that required them to report the transaction to the US Department of Commerce within 45 days. The civil penalty for failing to report such investment or acquisition can include a fine ranging from $2,500 to 25,000.00. This article will give the reader a brief overview of the initial reporting requirements.

I. The International Investment and Trade in Services Survey Act ("IITSSA")

The *International Investment and Trade in Services Survey Act* (IITSSA) is one of the primary US federal statutes that governs the reporting of investments made in the United States by foreign investors. Under

IITSSA, and its related regulations, a mandatory report is required of a US business enterprise when a foreign person acquires (directly or indirectly) through an existing US affiliate, a 10%+ voting interest in that enterprise, including an enterprise that results from the direct or indirect acquisition by a foreign person of a business segment or operating unit of an existing US business enterprise that is then organized as a separate legal entity, or · the existing US affiliate of a foreign person when it acquires a US business enterprise or operating unit that the existing US affiliate merges into its own operations.

The mandatory report must be filed with the US Department of Commerce's Bureau of Economic Analysis (the "BEA") no later than 45 days after the completion of such a transaction. Failure to file the mandatory report exposes one to a civil penalty of not less than $2,500.00, and not more than $25,000.00. Whoever willfully fails to report will be fined no more than $10,000.00. may be imprisoned, or both. Any officer, director, employee, or agent of any corporation who knowingly participates in such a violation, upon conviction, may be punished by a similar fine, imprisonment, or both. The IITSSA provides that the reported information is confidential, and may be used only for analytical or statistical purposes.

There is, however, an exemption for which an exemption claim must be filed if an established or acquired US business enterprise, as consolidated, has total assets of $3 million or less and does not own 200 acres or more of US land, or the total cost of an acquisition by an existing US affiliate of a US business enterprise or business segment or operating unit that it merges into its own operations is $3 million or less and does not involve purchase of 200 acres or more of US land. Additionally, no report need be filed if the transaction involves residential real estate held exclusively for personal use and not for profit making purposes.

A report may also be required of a US person who assists or intervenes in the sale to, or purchase by, a foreign person, of a 10 percent or more voting interest in a US business enterprise, including real estate, or who enters into a joint venture with a foreign person to create a US business enterprise. A US person must so report only if the US person knows of or has reason to believe that there is such foreign involvement.

II. The Exon-Florio Provision

The Exon-Florio provision provides for the review, investigation and possible suspension or blocking of certain mergers, acquisitions and takeovers that could threaten to impair US national security. The Committee on Foreign Investment in the United States ("CFIUS") has been delegated the authority to review and conduct investigations of mergers, acquisitions and takeovers where the transaction could result in foreign control of persons engaged in interstate commerce in the United States. Control refers to the ability to determine, direct or decide matters for the purchased company.

CFIUS has 30 days from notification of the transaction to review it and decide whether to proceed with an investigation. If the Committee determines that it should undertake an investigation, it must be completed within 45 days of this determination. Within 15 days after completion, the President must announce whether there is: (a) credible evidence that the purchaser might take action to impair the national security of the United States, and (b) that other provisions of law will not afford the President with adequate and appropriate authority to protect national security. If both of these criteria are met, the President may take action as the President considers appropriate to suspend or prohibit the transaction.

III. State Reporting Requirements

In additional to the Federal reporting requirements, many US states have reporting statutes affecting foreign investment. California, for example, has statutes on insurance and banking. New York has both reporting and taxation requirements specific to foreign fire insurance corporations. Illinois has reporting requirements for foreign persons owning agricultural land. However, Illinois recently eliminated many of the former special reporting requirements for foreign insurers. Arkansas likewise has a reporting requirement for foreign interests in agricultural land. These examples are not a comprehensive summary of all reporting statutes for the states listed. Instead, they should serve as indicators where statutes are known to exist. Areas covered in state reporting statutes are principally in agriculture and insurance, but the individual investor should investigate to determine what the local jurisdiction requires.

IV. Conclusion

Many foreign investors and business persons establishing operations in the United States, erroneously believe that their dealings with the US Federal and state governments will be limited to the acquisition of an L1 or E2 visa, and the filing of an annual US Federal Income Tax return. There are, however, several other important legal and financial formalities to observe if one is remain in compliance with the law and avoid exposure to civil penalties and criminal charges. Thus, our best advice is that it is always in the best interest of individuals contemplating an investment in the United States to engage the services of a US business lawyer and Certified Public Accountant with significant experience dealing with transnational matters, as early in the planning stages as possible, to help ensure compliance.

24

Criminal Admissibility and the "Sentencing Exception"

MYTH: If you have ever been convicted of a any criminal offence, you are automatically inadmissible to the United States and must apply for a waiver.

"Hello, Mr. Ortega, I need a waiver and I need it fast. I'm booked on a flight to Miami that leaves in a week to attend a convention, and I just found out that I'm inadmissible."

"Have you already been refused entry to the United States?"

"No, but—"

"Then what makes you think you're inadmissible?"

"Well, I have a criminal conviction."

"All right, we'll get to that in a second; why do you think that you're inadmissible?"

"A friend of mine told me that having a criminal conviction makes me automatically inadmissible. So I called the US embassy, and they confirmed it and said I would definitely need a waiver. They told me it would take 20 weeks to process, but I can't wait that long!"

"What was the conviction for?"

"Drunk driving."

"Is that your only conviction?"

"Yes."

"What was the sentence?"

"Three years probations, plus I had to pay a fine and go to traffic school."

"Anything else?"

"No, that's it."

Our offices in San Francisco and London receive frantic telephone calls like the one quoted above on almost a daily basis, from people about to embark on a trip to the United States who have been told that they are inadmissible to the United States because of a past criminal conviction. By the time we speak with them, many of these people are almost resigned to canceling their travel plans.

These individuals have been told by their employers, their colleagues, or even the US embassy that their single criminal conviction makes them inadmissible and that they must apply for a waiver—which could take from 6 months to a year to process. That's when the panic sets in. Airline tickets have already been purchase, and hotel rooms reserved; friends and family are eagerly awaiting at the other end. "Isn't there a faster way to get a waiver?" they ask.

In fact, many individuals may not be inadmissible at all regardless of their conviction. Or if they are, they may qualify for what is known as the "petty theft" exception set out in section 212 of the Immigration and Nationality Act ("the Act').

According to the Act, a noncitizen who has been convicted, or who admits the essential elements, of a crime involving moral turpitude ("CMT") is inadmissible. Thus, the first thing to consider is whether ones conviction falls under the CMT category or not. By way of example, a single drunk driving conviction does not fall under this category, and does not render one inadmissible. In other words, a waiver is not required in this circumstance. However, the question of whether a particular offence is or is not a CMT requires some research.

If research reveals that one has been convicted of even a single CMT, then one is clearly inadmissible under the Act.. However the Act sets out an exception that has come to be known as the *sentencing exception* (formerly known as the *petty offence exception*). To qualify for the *sentencing exception*, an applicant for admission to the United States must show:

a.) he or she committed only one crime;

b.) the maximum penalty possible for the crime did not exceed imprisonment for one year; and

c.) the noncitizen seeking admission was not sentenced to a term of imprisonment longer than 6 months.

Clearly, the only way to determine whether one meets the above elements of the exception requires an examination of both the conviction documents and the underlying law of the offence.

The good news is that if one satisfies the requirements of the *sentencing exception*, one may enter the United States without first visiting the embassy or enduring the lengthy and onerous burden of applying for a waiver.

Ultimately, the decision to admit or not to admit in such a case lies entirely in the hands of the inspecting officer at the US port of entry. This officer is the person that must be convinced whether or not one is admissible under section 212 of the Act. Thus, it is essential that one be armed with the evidence and (preferably) the applicable legal authority.

25

Myths Associates with Arrests, Cautions, and Convictions

Myth 1: "Our employee has a criminal record. He is therefore required to apply for a visa before travelling to the United States."

The Reality: It depends on the record.

This myth most commonly arises in relation to Question B on the Electronic System for Travel Authorization ("ESTA") required to travel to the United States. Question B asks:

Have you ever been arrested or convicted for an offense or crime involving moral turpitude or a violation related to a controlled substance; or have been arrested or convicted for two or more offenses for which the aggregate sentence to confinement was five years or more; or have been a controlled substance trafficker; or are you seeking entry to engage in criminal or immoral activities?

When one answers "yes" to Question B, US Customs and Border Protection reviews the application and determines whether travel will be authorized or whether the traveller must apply for a visa at the United States Embassy or Consulate abroad before travelling to the United States.

The portion of the question that generally causes confusion is whether the arrest or conviction was for a crime involving moral turpitude ("CIMT").

Common law in the United States defines moral turpitude ambiguously as "conduct which is inherently base, vile, or depraved, and contrary to the accepted rules of morality and the duties owed between persons or to society in general." Further, the punishment imposed does not shed any light as to the presence or absence of moral turpitude. For example, some crimes punishable by only a fine may be considered crimes involving moral turpitude, whilst other crimes generally considered by the general public to be serious are not.

The determination as to whether a "foreign arrest or conviction" involves moral turpitude requires a comparison of the subject criminal record against both the equivalent United States federal or state criminal statutes and the relevant United States immigration laws.

Our firm recommends that you consult with a US-qualified business immigration lawyer before instructing the subject employee to complete the ESTA questionnaire or contacting the United States Embassy or Consulate to schedule an appointment for a visa application. The United States Embassy or Consulate does not advise in advance as to whether it will consider a particular arrest or conviction to be a CIMT. Only a qualified business immigration lawyer with substantial experience dealing with issues of criminal inadmissibility will be able to provide insight into this in advance of the consular appointment, and will be able to assess the likelihood of success in such an application.

It is quite common for an individual that legally could have answered "no" to Question B, to nevertheless book a visa interview, either because he is uncertain about the definition of CIMT, or because he directly consults with the DOS call center and is instructed to do so. At the visa interview, even if the attending officer is unable to find that the arrest, caution or conviction is a CIMT, she may nevertheless deny the visa application on other grounds, such as "medical inadmissibility" in the case of a Drink-Drive arrest, or for the less comprehensible "insufficient ties outside of the United States." A visa denial on these grounds will render the individual who would have otherwise received ESTA approval unable to travel on the Visa Waiver Program. Furthermore, the visa denial remains on one's DOS record for life and is quite difficult to overcome in a future application, as embassy officials typically defer to the previous denial unless there has been a material change of circumstances.

Myth 2: *"Our employee's criminal conviction is now spent (or expunged) so he does not need to disclose it to the US immigration service or to the Embassy of the United States."*

The Reality: The United States government does not recognize the concept of spent convictions.

An arrest or conviction that falls under a category requiring disclosure must be revealed, regardless of how long ago it occurred and regardless of whether it has been removed from one's record.

26

UK Police Cautions/Warnings and US Immigration Law

The way in which US immigration law treats criminal matters for purposes of determining a non-US citizen's admissibility to the United States is complex. Notably, travellers from the United Kingdom are often surprised that a UK police caution or formal warning, in which there was no court or judge involvement and no filing of formal criminal charges, could render them "inadmissible" to the United States *for any reason.*

Their astonishment arises not only from the complex intersection of criminal and US immigration law, but also from the fact that the US Department of State has not been consistent in the way it treats UK cautions/warnings, adopting a new approach as recently as 2014. The recent 2014 policy, described below, could mean that non-US citizens with UK cautions who were previously traveling to the United States without issue may now be barred from the United States, unless eligible for an exemption or waiver of inadmissibility.

Below is a brief summary of the current state of UK police cautions/warnings and US immigration law. This article demonstrates that the prudent approach would be to treat all formal UK police cautions and warnings as "admissions" for purposes of determining criminal inadmissibility, unless there is evidence showing that the admission was not obtained in compliance with controlling US legal precedent.

I. Overview of Criminal Inadmissibility under INA § 212(a)(2)

An alien is inadmissible to the United States for committing a "crime involving moral turpitude" (CIMT) or a crime involving a controlled substance, including an attempt or conspiracy to commit them, if (1) the individual was convicted of such crime; **or** (2) the individual *admitted* to having committed such a crime, or admitted to its essential elements.

Further, (3) if the US immigration official has a mere *reason* to believe the alien was or is involved in the *trafficking of* a controlled substance (e.g., intent to sell), the alien can be rendered inadmissible under INA § 212(a)(2)(C)(i), even though the alien was not convicted (e.g., acquitted) of the crime and has not admitted to its commission or essential factual elements.

A finding of criminal inadmissibility is not the end of the road. Once an individual is considered to be inadmissible, he or she should then pursue, through legal counsel, any applicable exemption or waiver of inadmissibility for the US visa type being sought.

II. UK Cautions/Warnings Defined

Below are three UK out-of-court dispositions particularly relevant to US immigration law:

i) Simple Police Caution. A simple caution is a formal notice from a police officer that a person has committed an offence. Under current policy, the individual will generally be fingerprinted and photographed. The police will likely offer a caution if it is a minor offence and usually if there is no other criminal history. **The police can only issue a simple caution if the person** *admits* **to the offence** and agrees to be cautioned. If the person refuses the caution (e.g., denies the offence), then formal criminal charges may be brought against the individual.

ii) Conditional Police Caution. A conditional police caution is the same as a simple caution in all respects, **including an** *admission* **to the offence**, except the individual is subject to certain conditions. Failure to comply with the conditions will result in formal criminal charges being brought against the individual.

iii) Cannabis Warnings. A cannabis warning is not a caution, but a verbal warning by a police officer to a first-time offender possessing a small amount of cannabis for personal use. The police cannot give the formal verbal warning **unless the suspect** *admits* **ownership of the cannabis**. The police officer will record that the suspect admitted to owning the cannabis and the suspect will be asked to sign this record. Such warnings will show up on an ACRO report and will need to be addressed for purposes of US immigration.

The consistent element in all of these UK out-of-court dispositions is that the individual must "admit" to the offence. As discussed below, whether the admission under UK law qualifies as an admission under US immigration law requires a case-by-case analysis.

III. UK Cautions/Warnings Are Not "Convictions"

A "conviction" for purposes of US immigration requires (i) a formal judgment of guilt entered by a court; (ii) or if adjudication is withheld: a finding of guilt by a judge or jury, a plea of guilty or *nolo contendere* by the alien, or admission of facts from the alien sufficient for a finding of guilty; or (iii) the imposition of some form of punishment by a judge.

Based on this definition, UK police cautions or warnings do not qualify as convictions for purposes of US immigration. On April 9, 2014, the US Department of State's Visa Office agreed. The reasoning being that there is no official court or judicial action. However, as explained below, the absence of a "conviction" does not preclude a finding of criminal inadmissibility for purposes of US immigration.

IV. UK Police Cautions/Warnings Can Be "Admissions"

If there is no conviction on the applicant's record, the immigration official can nevertheless consider the applicant inadmissible to the USA if the applicant "admitted" to committing the crime or its essential factual elements. Such an admission may have been elicited by a police officer, federal law enforcement official, judge, medical doctor, or US immigration official.

i.) An "admission" for purposes of US Immigration Law.

The legal criteria for an "admission" for purposes of INA § 212(a)(2) is defined as follows in Matter of K: the alien must (1) prior to the admission be given an adequate definition of the crime, including all essential elements; (2) admit to conduct that constitutes the essential elements of the crime; and (3) provide an admission that is explicit, unqualified, voluntary and unequivocal. There is no requirement that the alien admit the legal conclusion or non-factual elements of the crime.

Formal criminal charges are not required for there to be a valid admission. For example, in 2013, in a highly-publicized UK fraud trial against the former assistants of UK celebrity chef Nigella Lawson, Ms. Lawson admitted under oath to having used cocaine seven times and "smok[ing] the odd joint." She denied ever being a habitual drug user or addict. Even though Scotland Yard never brought criminal charges against Ms. Lawson for her admitted drug use, and does not intend to do so, on March 30, 2014, British Airways refused to allow Ms. Lawson to board a plane for her holiday to the United States, presumably at the request of the US government. The US government did not explicitly release the exact reason for its refusal to admit Ms. Lawson to the United States[9]; however, a reasonable analysis of US immigration law's approach to controlled substance violations shows that her highly-publicized *admission* in court to having violated a controlled substance law is consistent with a finding of inadmissibility, provided that the other elements of Matter of K were met in eliciting her admission. In short, an admission made in the course and scope of a trial can have the unintended effect of rendering the person making the admission inadmissible to the United States, even when no criminal charges are ever pending against that individual.

That said, an admission *need not* have been made under oath to render an individual inadmissible. For example, an admission made to an immigration official during a visa interview could be enough for a non-appealable finding of inadmissibility, as long as they elicit the admission pursuant to <u>Matter of K</u>. If <u>Matter of K</u> was not followed, a finding of inadmissibility should be challenged.

Further, an admission by an alien to a medical doctor during a required medical exam for a US immigrant visa or "green card" that the applicant had smoked marijuana could be a basis for rendering an alien inadmissible to the United States on the basis of having admitted to violating a controlled substance law, provided the doctor obtained the admission in accordance with <u>Matter of K</u>. Again, if <u>Matter of K</u> was not followed, a finding of inadmissibility should be challenged.

Interestingly, if an admission is made subsequent to (i) a valid acquittal/dismissal of criminal charges or (ii) a valid pardon of a *conviction*, the subsequent admission by itself will **not** generally render the person thereby inadmissible. However, if the criminal charges were related to the trafficking of a controlled substance (e.g., intent to sell), an admission following an acquittal/dismissal of the charges could nevertheless provide the US immigration official with "reason to believe" that the offence occurred and render the applicant inadmissible, notwithstanding the court's disposition.

ii) UK Police Cautions/Warnings as "Admissions"

For an individual to receive a formal UK caution or cannabis warning under current policy, the individual <u>must</u> admit the offence to the police officer. In order for there to be a finding of inadmissibility based on the admission: (1) the criminal offence must be a CIMT or controlled substance violation, as defined by US regulations, and (2) the admission to the UK police officer must comply with the requirements set forth in the Matter of K.

The US Department of State's policy regarding UK police cautions has not been consistent. On September 23, 1997, there was an Advisory Opinion from the Dept. of State that stated UK police cautions were "not an admission" for purposes of US immigration law.

In late 2013, the US Embassy in London requested new guidance from the US Department of State and began placing visa applications in which the applicant had UK police cautions in "administrative processing" until the new advisory opinion was released.

In February 2014, the Embassy began adjudicating the on-hold "UK caution cases" consistent with convictions and admissions. Although this implied that the US Department of State had issued its new formal advisory opinion to the US Embassy in London, the opinion has not been released to the public.

In April 2014, the US Department of State clarified to the American Immigration Lawyers Association that, although UK cautions are not convictions, they can still be "admissions" for purposes of inadmissibility, appearing to depart from its prior 1997 opinion. The Dept. of State stated that there must be a "case-by-case" determination, presumably because UK police officers are not trained in eliciting Matter of K admissions or US immigration law.

The US Dept. of State implied that a "case by case" analysis is required to determine whether, for example, the UK police policy at the time of the caution required an admission for the issuance of the caution, an adequate definition of the crime was provided to the individual prior to its issuance, or whether the admission was voluntary.

The US Dept. of State's current policy appears to treat UK cautions as admissions, unless this type of evidence can be provided to show insufficient compliance with the Matter of K.

The current policy also means that individuals with UK police cautions who have traveled to the United States based on the Dept. of State's 1997 policy may now need to obtain an exemption or waiver of inadmissibility in order to return to the United States.

It is important to note that even if a UK caution or warning is "spent" for purposes of UK law, it remains on the individual's record under US immigration law: the mere elapsing of time does not remove a formal police caution or warning for purposes of criminal inadmissibility determinations.

V. Exemptions and Waivers of Criminal Inadmissibility

A finding of criminal inadmissibility is not the end of the road for a potential traveler to the United States. Depending on the visa being sought and crime(s) at issue, the applicant may be eligible for an exemption or a waiver of inadmissibility. The applicant should arrive fully prepared at his or her interview at the US embassy/consulate with succinct legal arguments and supporting documentation in favor of such exemption or waiver of inadmissibility applications.

VI. Conclusion

Considering the way in which the US Embassy in London is now treating UK cautions, the prudent approach would be to anticipate that the Embassy will treat an individual's UK caution as an "admission", unless there is evidence showing that compliance with Matter of K was deficient. Because UK cautions are never "spent" for purposes of US immigration law, this new policy may have the effect of rendering previously authorized travelers to the United States inadmissible, absent an exemption or waiver application that was not previously necessary.

Criminal matters must be carefully addressed and analyzed before attempting to travel to the United States. The intersection of criminal law and US immigration law is complicated, requiring first an analysis of whether the crime at issue falls into the definition of a "CIMT" or "controlled substance" violation; whether there exists a "conviction", "admission", or – if applicable – "reason to believe"; and if so, whether any applicable exemption or waiver of inadmissibility can be pursued. It is advisable to seek legal counsel to properly assess and, if needed, to seek relief from these complex criminal inadmissibility grounds.

About the Author

Ortega-Medina & Associates are a respected multinational law firm practicing exclusively in the field of corporate and business US immigration law. The firm is proud of its streamlined and eco-friendly paperless case processing system, which allows it to provide its clients with creative and highly personalized strategies in the processing of their US business immigration and employment-based US business visa applications.

The firm offers a full range of legal representation to corporate HR departments, foreign investors, and high net-worth individuals seeking to establish a business foothold in the United States, or to secure visas for key employees or new foreign workers. To this end, its team of legal professionals actively manages the immigration portfolio of qualifying organizations and individuals, including processing visas for professionals, multinational executives & managers, investors, and persons of extraordinary and exceptional ability.

Printed in Poland
by Amazon Fulfillment
Poland Sp. z o.o., Wrocław

53117549R00076